STURMARTILLERIE CREWMAN

Sturmgeschütze, Panzerjäger, and Panzerartillerie

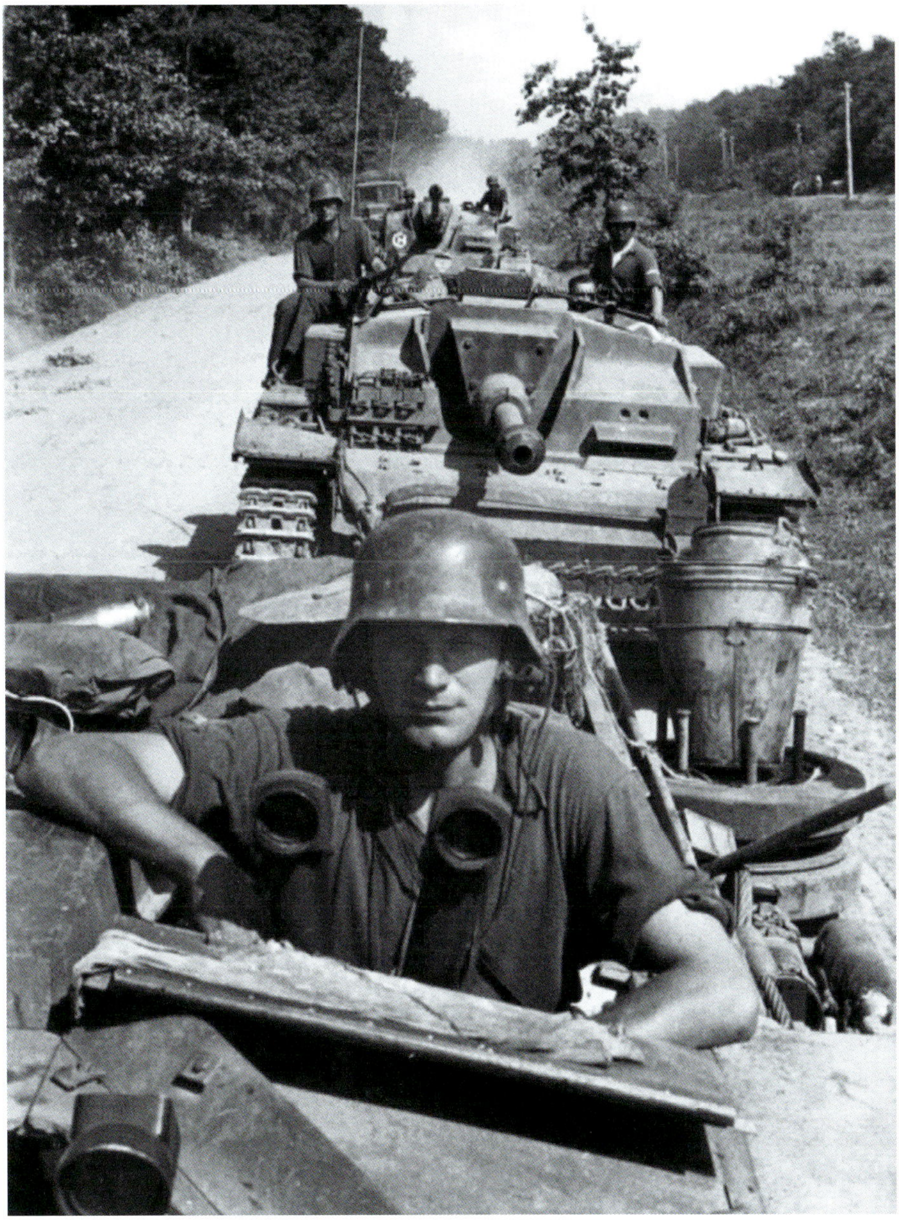

SIMON FORTY &
RICHARD CHARLTON TAYLOR

CASEMATE | ILLUSTRATED

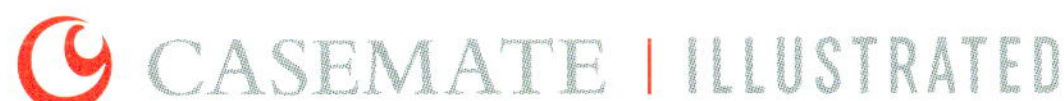

CIS0051

Published in 2025 by
CASEMATE PUBLISHERS
1950 Lawrence Road, Havertown, PA 19083, USA
and
47 Church Street, Barnsley, S70 2AS, UK

Print Edition: ISBN 978-1-63624-516-4
Digital Edition: ISBN 978-1-63624-517-1

Design by Eleanor Forty-Robbins
Printed and bound in the Czech Republic by FINIDR s.r.o.

CASEMATE PUBLISHERS (US)
Telephone (610) 853-9131
Fax (610) 853-9146
Email: casemate@casematepublishers.com
www.casematepublishers.com

CASEMATE PUBLISHERS (UK)
Telephone (0)1226 734350
Email: casemate@casemateuk.com
www.casemateuk.com

Author's note: All photos credited on the captions. The authors thank all those who have contributed, in particular Ruth Sheppard and her team at Casemate for helpful and constructive assistance, Eleanor Forty-Robbins (design), Mark Franklin (artwork), Michael Leventhal of Greenhill Publishing for permission to quote from Bruno Bork and Friedrich Sander, and for their help with illustrations and other material: Christian Ankerstjerne (panzerworld.com), Marek at Panzernet, Mike Holverson at www.themarshalsbaton.com, Michel Blinoff (Kubinka Tank Museum photos), Kurtis Lowden at The Australian Armour and Artillery Museum, Neil Powell at Battlefieldhistorian.com, Ian Spring of Pixpast.com, Marc Romanych of Digitalhistoryarchive.com, Jari Saurio at Parola (photographs courtesy Parolan Panssarimuseo—the Parola Armor Museum—Finland), and last but not least, the generosity of Akira Takiguchi. If we've omitted anyone in error, please let us know through the publisher. We'd like to recommend the following websites that helped greatly with our research: allworldwars.com/German-English-Military-Dictionary.html; feldgrau.com; kriegsfunker.com; lexikon-der-wehrmacht.de; lonesentry.com; panzerworld.com; track-link.com; and waralbum.ru.

Vehicle names present a problem. Today we describe vehicles with names that were not used at the time—but the German propensity for using long descriptive designations, changing them multiple times, renaming everything on a regular basis and then going with whatever Hitler liked best makes it easy to get mixed up. We've tried to be consistent but have erred on the side of clarity rather than exactitude. For detailed analysis of all the names and designations one need look no further than the brilliant Panzer Tracts series by Hilary L. Doyle & Thomas L. Jentz.

The Publisher's authorised representative in the EU for product safety is Authorised Rep Compliance Ltd., Ground Floor, 71 Lower Baggot Street, Dublin D02 P593, Ireland.
www.arccompliance.com

Title page: The commander's station on a StuG 40 Ausf G without a cupola. The commander's Scherenfernrohr 14Z and the gunner's periscope are in evidence. Note the helmet—unusual but not exceptional; wearing a helmet was difficult inside the vehicle or when headphones were necessary. (GF Collection)

Map: German military map of Stalingrad-Süd—on September 28, 1942, a German soldier was able to write in his diary that his division had taken the southern part of the city and reached the Volga, but not without a fight: five square miles took three weeks of heading fighting; tanks and StuGs were heavily used in the urban fighting. (LoC)

Above right: This smart *Gefreiter* wears the *feldgrau* uniform of the *Sturmartillerie* with what looks like *Totenköpfe* in his *Kragenspiegel*. As artillerymen were more likely to recce on foot, it was felt that *feldgrau* was better camouflage than Panzer black. At the front, however, particularly in winter, camouflaged clothing was often preferred. The wraparound jacket—designed to reduce snags in the confines of a *Sturmgeschütz*—stood out in a crowd and was, apparently, helpful romantically! (RCT)

Contents

Timeline of Events 4

Introduction 10

The Soldier 30

The Vehicles 52

Crew Duties 88

The Units 103

Mobility 111

Tactics 118

Conclusion 126

Further Reading 127

Index 128

Timeline of Events

In 1935 Oberst Erich von Manstein raised the idea of an SP gun to assist the infantry in battalions integrated into infantry divisions. In June the following year, after approval by the General Staff, the order was given to develop an armored infantry support vehicle mounting at least a 7.5 cm gun. The project was passed to the artillery under the supervision of the General Staff's Technical Section 8, then under the aegis of Oberst Walter Model. A year later in 1937 five prototypes were built. Trials of what would become the StuG III (vehicle by Daimler-Benz; gun by Krupp) began on the Kummersdorf ranges, while the Artillery School at Jüterbog's Experimental Battery began trials with the Infantry Demonstration Regiment at Doberitz. Alkett was founded in Berlin as a subsidiary of Rheinmetall-Borsig AG and would become the main producer of the StuG III. From then on, with initial deployment in May 1940 during the campaign in the West, the SPGs of the *Sturmgeschütze*, *Panzerjäger*, and *Panzerartillerie* would go on to become a Wehrmacht staple, mixing and matching AFV chassis (many foreign), engines, armor, and weapons systems in the never-ending quest for bigger and better. The irony is that SPG production, despite Allied air raids, only really hit its straps in the last year of the war—in May 1944 Jagdpanzer IV production took over from PzKpfw IVs on the Vomag production lines—and specifically in the last few months of the war, when, for example, 930 PzKpfw IV/70(V)s were produced between August 1944 and March 1945. A staggering 7,720 StuG 40 Ausf Gs were built.

January–March 1940: Alkett produce 30 Gepanzerter Selbstfahrlafette für Sturmgeschütz 7.5 cm Kanone Ausf As. The SdKfz 142 utilizes much of the PzKpfw III's basic hull shape as well as its suspension and drivetrain.

February 1940: First StuG IIIs issued to troops. By end May Sturmartillerie-Batterien 640, 659, 660, and 665 deploy vehicles in the fighting in France.

February 1940: Alkett converts 38 PzKpfw I Ausf Bs to carry the 15 cm sIG 33. They fight in the campaign in the West.

March 1940: Daimler-Benz and Skoda convert over 200 PzKpfw I Ausf Bs to carry the 4.7 cm PaK(t), creating the Panzerjäger I.

June 1940: Alkett produces the first StuG III Ausf B. It will see action in the Balkans and *Barbarossa*.

March 31, 1941: Hitler is presented with the prototypes of the 10.5 cm K18 auf Panzer Selbstfahrlafette IVa (nicknamed "Dicker Max"). It doesn't enter production.

May–September 1941: Alkett produces the StuG III Ausf C and D, most go to replace losses in Russia.

June 1941: *Barbarossa* highlights the ineffectiveness of the German tanks against the heavier Soviet tanks. Immediately discussions start about the production of stopgap *Panzerjäger*.

July 1941: Alkett ordered to produce chassis to take the 15 cm sIG 33. This leads to the short-run Sturminfanteriegeschütz 33B.

September 1941: First StuG III Ausf Es produced: this will be the first major production run with 272 produced up to March 1942.

September 28, 1941: OKW orders that StuGs be produced with a larger gun and more armor. The result is the SdKfz 142/1—the Ausf F—employing the StuK 40 L/43. The first is produced in March 1943. The last 31 of 359 produced receive the L/48 gun that becomes standard on the F/8.

November–December 1941: A total of 12 15 cm sIG 33 auf Fahrgestell PzKpfw II SPGs are produced. They are sent to North Africa early in 1942.

December 1941: A development order leads to the first prototype in March 1942 of the 10.5 cm Sturmhaubitze 42 (SdKfz 142/2) produced by Alkett.

December 1941: BMM is given the order to produce a *Panzerjäger* on the PzKpfw 38(t) chassis. The result is the Marder III (SdKfz 139) of which nearly 350 are converted.

December 20, 1941: Alkett receives an order for an SPG using captured 7.62 cm PaK 36(r) guns. Some are mounted on Lorraine Schleppers; over 200 are placed on converted PzKpfw II Ausf Ds to produce the Marder II (SdKfz 132).

March 1942: Two prototypes of the 12.8 cm Selbstfahrlafette L/61 are built on the Henschel VK 30.01 chassis. The "Sturer Emil" doesn't enter production.

June 1942: PzKpfw II tank construction is replaced by mounting on its chassis either the 7.5 cm PaK 40/2 (Marder II, SdKfz 131) or the 10.5 cm leFH 18M L/24 (SdKfz 124 Wespe).

Below right: Waffen-SS Grille Ausf H showing the gun traveling lock and the driver's two vision slots. In the Ausf M the gun lock changed, and the driver had a separate compartment as the gun and armor plate were pushed back. (GF Collection)

StuH 42 bombing up—note two-piece 10.5 cm ammo. With so many StuGs being used in the *Panzerjäger* role, the infantry support requirement needed filling. The StuH was intended to do that. (Bundesarchiv, Bild 1011-220-0838-18/Harschneck/CC-BY-SA 3.0)

July 1942: The first batch of Lorraine Schleppers are converted to become *Panzerjäger* carrying the PaK 40/1 L/46 gun—the SdKfz 135. Most go to units in France. Further use of the Schlepper see conversions to carry the 15 cm sFH 13/1 and 10.5 cm leFH 18. Similar work is done to the captured Hotchkiss H39s to carry the 7.5 cm PaK 40 and the leFH 18. The same to FCM 36 tanks—to carry the leFH 16 and, in 1943 the PaK 40.

September 1942: The Ausf F/8 starts production with an improved hull and increase in armor protection. Demand is so great that Alkett stops making the PzKpfw III and turns over completely to the StuG III, converting those PzKpfw III hulls that are in production.

November 1942: The first 7.5 cm PaK 40/3 auf Panzerkampfwagen 38(t) Ausf H (SdKfz 138) is produced. Over 400 of this version of the Marder III will see action.

November 1942: Krupp produces eight 10.5 cm leFH 18/1 (Sf) auf Geschützwagen IVb prototypes with open-topped turrets that can traverse 70°. The design loses out to Alkett's Wespe.

December 1942: The definitive StuG version, the StuG 40 Ausf G, of which 7,720 will be built, uses the F/8 hull but includes a cupola for the commander and an armored shield for the MG in front of the loader's hatch. Most are built by Alkett, but MIAG produce a quantity of the run.

February 1943: The first production model of the 15 cm schweres Infanteriegeschütz 33 (sf) auf PzKpfw 38(t) Ausf H delivered. 90 of the SdKfz 138/1 Grille enter service in early 1943. Another 280 will be produced in 1943 and 1944 on the PzKpfw 38(t) Ausf M chassis.

February 1943: The first of nearly 500 Hornisse (8.8 cm PaK43/1 L/71 auf Fahrgestell PzKpfw III/IV) are produced by Deutsche-Eisernwerke. It's renamed Nashorn by Hitler.

February 6, 1943: Hitler orders production of 90 Ferdinands—Sturmgeschütz mit 8.8 cm PaK 43/2. The result is the SdKfz 184 produced by Nibelungenwerke.

March 1943: First of c. 1,200 Sturmhaubitze delivered.

March 1943: First of 975 Marder IIIs mounting the PaK 40/3 on a PzKpfw 38(t) Ausf M is produced.

April 1943: The first of around 300 Sturmpanzer IVs is manufactured by Deutsche Eisenwerke. The SdKfz 166 is nicknamed *Brummbär* by the Allies and mounts a 15 cm StuH 43 on the PzKpfw IV chassis.

July 5, 1943: The battle of Kursk begins. It's been postponed so that new weapons, the Panther and Ferdinand, can take part.

October 1943: Introduction of the *Topfblende* (nicknamed the *Saukopf*) gun mantlet for the StuG III.

October, November 23 and 16, 1943: Major Allied air attacks impact on Alkett's StuG production. This leads to Krupp-Gruson's StuG IV. Alkett gets back up to speed by acquiring a factory in Falkensee.

December 1943: Testing begins on the Jagdpanzer 38(t)—today we call it the Hetzer. Over 2,500 are produced by BMM and Skoda April 1944–May 1945.

December 16, 1943: First prototype Jagdpanther shown to Hitler. Nearly 400 SdKfz 173s will be manufactured by MIAG and MNH between January 1944 and March 1945.

December 1943: The first-production StuG IV mounting the 7.5 cm StuK 40 L/48 joins 30 conversions from PzKpfw IV chassis. Over 1,100 SdKfz 167s will be produced by Krupp-Gruson.

Early 1944 A coaxial MG is introduced to the StuG III.

January 1944: Vomag produces the first of over 750 Jagdpanzer IVs (SdKfz 162) mounting the 7.5 cm PaK 39 L/48.

February 1944: Hitler's end-of-1943 suggestion that the Ferdinand should be renamed Elefant is made official.

Spring 1944: *Nahverteidigung* and remote-controlled MG introduced to the StuG III.

July 1944: The first of 77 Jagdtigers rolls off the Nibelungenwerke production line. The SdKfz 186 mounts a 12.8 cm PaK 44 L/55.

August 1944: Vomag starts building the PzKpfw IV/70(V). At the same time the Alkett-designed IV/70(A) is produced at the Nibelungenwerke. Both mount the PaK 42 L/70.

October 17, 1944: The Nibelungenwerke is heavily bombed and most production is outsourced.

April 25, 1945: A bombing raid destroys 50 percent of the Skoda Works buildings and 30 percent of the equipment. In microcosm it's the same story around the Third Reich and heralds the end of German AFV production.

Panzer Helfen Dir!

Armor Helps You!

The German Army produced leaflets to inform its soldiers. Subtitled "What the grenadier needs to know about armored fighting vehicles," this leaflet of September 15, 1944, set out the main characteristics of German AFVs in the popular, easily digestible style used in the *Panther/Tiger-Fibel* primers. It grouped AFVs into six categories—*Panzer* (tanks), *Sturmgeschütze* (assault guns), *Panzerspähwagen* (armored scout cars), *Schützen-Panzerwagen* (APCs), *Panzerjäger* (tank hunters), and *Selbstfahrlafetten* (SPGs). These are edited excerpts from the leaflet. They identify what this book covers.

Sturmgeschütz
Strengths: It's very low and mobile. It has strong frontal armor. It's accurate to 2,000 m and its gun can knock out most enemy tanks up to this range. Its effect with HE shells on infantry targets is devastating (ricochets allow air bursts!). It gives your attack and counterattack power and momentum.

Weaknesses: It has neither a rotating turret nor a built-in machine gun. So, when it has to change its angle of attack it has to shift 100 percent of its 22-tonne weight—whereas a Tiger only moves its turret, that's 8 tonnes, 14 percent of its weight. It only shoots straight ahead. When buttoned up, visibility is very limited. It is almost defenseless against close-range attacks. Sides and rear are vulnerable. It can only carry limited ammunition and fuel. It is particularly vulnerable to terrain difficulties (swamps, dense forests, towns, watercourses).

Tasks: It should help you in the attack. That's what it's built for, and nothing else. It pounces on enemy tanks that try to stop your attack and destroys them. It destroys strongpoints that offer you tough resistance. As a clenched fist, assault guns force a break-in at a crucial point. In defense they are the iron reserve of strength for counterattacks.

To sum up: The *Sturmgeschütz* is **not** a tank because it has neither a turret nor a built-in machine gun; **not** an infantry gun—it doesn't have its 300 hp to only change position twice a week; **not** a bunker, because it should use its impact force; **not** a radio station, because otherwise two men and a gun would be redundant; **not** an emergency helper for technical and medical issues because it's more important in the front line; **not** a snowplow because it is neither suitable nor intended for that purpose.

Note: The *Sturmgeschütz* is also used as a tank destroyer. So take a look at the *Tank Destroyer* chapter!

Panzerjäger
There are three types:

- **PaK Sf:** Antitank gun mounted on self-propelled chassis [such as Nashorn]. Different to SPGs only because of their weapon—higher penetrating power—and through their optics—better direct sights. Otherwise, strengths and weaknesses are the same as those of the SPG. Long range and accuracy must compensate for weak armor. So, don't use as a tank!

- ***Sturmgeschütze:*** You can hardly tell the difference when they are used as tank destroyers or as assault guns. But as a *Panzerjäger* your job is primarily to hunt tanks. How this task can best be solved is left to the leader of the *Panzerjäger* unit.
- **Designated *Panzerjäger* vehicles:** Jagdpanzer 38, Jagdpanzer IV, PzKpfw IV long, Jagdpanther, and Jagdtiger.

Either by stalking or lying in wait, individual hunts or group operations, the *Panzerjäger* always supports you, even if he doesn't stay in your attack lane. Remember, he's a hunter. He hunts your most dangerous enemies.

Selbstfahrlafetten

A field howitzer with its tractor is over 10 m long and needs at least 5 minutes to get ready to fire or to change firing positions. An SPG is 4.80 m long and is always ready to fire. If it wants to change position or the position gets too hot, the driver presses the accelerator and off she goes!

The self-propelled howitzer is a much smaller target, much more mobile, and always ready to fire. But it only has light armor protection, a small amount of ammunition, and limited offroad capability.

But, a self-propelled gun ... is not a tank. Its protective armor may be the same as eight steel helmets in a row ... but its front is 175 times larger.

Tasks: They are mobile artillery! They must quickly follow tank attacks and be able to suddenly shift the focus of fire this way and that ... but only where there is a need and there are no armor-piercing weapons. They can open up and engage in direct fire only if they have strong fire protection from tanks because they are completely open at the top and back.

Don't expect them to help you like a tank. A heavy SPG has less than a quarter of the ammunition that a Tiger carries. If you are working with SPGs, stay away from them: they will draw fire. Support them against all threats as best you can. If they fail, they will no longer be of any help to you. Your comrades on an SPG are not protected much better than you, and they sit almost 1.5 m higher. Bear this in mind!

Introduction

As early as 1927 the Reichswehr started looking at developing a self-propelled (SP) gun to accompany infantry during attacks. It did not lead to anything but Oberst Erich Manstein, as he was then—he of later Chir River and Kharkov fame—was the man who came up with a plan that would see him being dubbed "*Vater der Sturmartillerie*."

In 1935 he raised a memorandum to Generaloberst Ludwig Beck, *Chef des Generalstabes des Heeres*, and Generaloberst Werner von Fritsch, *Oberbefehlshaber des Heeres*, about the need of the infantry for an armored vehicle that would be deployed to knock out strongpoints: pillboxes, machine-gun nests, and the obstacles that had caused the German *Stoßtruppen* of 1918 so much difficulty. Manstein proposed that each infantry division had a battalion of these vehicles—he called them *Sturmartillerie*—made up of three batteries of six guns each.

His ideas met with immediate approval, so he produced another memorandum to Beck dated June 8, 1936, outlining his plans in more detail. He emphasized the separation and difference between tanks and *Sturmartillerie*: that tanks were there to break through the enemy infantry zone and use their speed to reach the areas behind, while the *Sturmartillerie* was to fight alongside the infantry. He emphasized that tank units would fight as mixed units of all weapons, alongside supporting motorized artillery, and with motorized infantry and technical troops to ensure success could be exploited. Tanks would be used en masse to provide a spearhead.

On the other hand, *Sturmartillerie* was an auxiliary weapon of the normal infantry division. In attack it would be used as escort batteries; in defense it should be able to perform as the artillery and fire indirectly to 7 km. *Sturmartillerie* should carry the infantry attack forward by eliminating dangerous targets with direct fire. It wouldn't fight in large numbers like the tanks, but in smaller units so as not to become a target of enemy artillery.

However, he added that *Sturmartillerie* vehicles must be able to engage enemy tanks, using their strengths—low height and suitability for ambush—rather than depend on armor as a defense.

Gen. Erich von Manstein was pivotal in the creation of the Sturmgeschütz in the early 1930s when still an *Oberst*. He's seen here near Kerch, Ukraine in May 1942 during his 11. Armee's successful battle for the peninsula. (NAC)

Manstein posited that the *Sturmartillerie* unit in an infantry division should be a detachment with three battalions and six guns and could replace the light artillery detachment or the divisional armored detachment. *Sturmartillerie* personnel should be trained as part of the artillery, but also—so they could learn their tasks as an accompanying battalion—as part of the infantry. Above all, this proposal should be implemented immediately, and the infantry should start training with mockups.

Shortly after sending his memorandum, Manstein received a response. It broadly agreed with him and placed no objections in the way of experimentation but highlighted (a) that the direct fire required for close infantry support need only be to a range of 4 km as an infantry weapon didn't need the range of a divisional artillery piece, (b) that *Sturmartillerie* had to be able to fully take over the tasks of the tank destroyer.

The day before the date of this memorandum, June 15, 1936, the Heereswaffenamt, the Army Weapons Office or HWA, was authorized to design a turretless, open-topped armored fighting vehicle (AFV) no taller than a standing man and which should have at least a 7.5 cm main gun that could achieve a range of 6,000 m. Daimler-Benz AG was given the job of designing the vehicle and Krupp the gun.

Daimler-Benz AG chose to use its PzKpfw III chassis and components as the basis for the experimental "0" series of five prototypes. Krupp provided a short-barreled 7.5 cm Sturmkanone (StuK) gun.

Unfortunately for the speedy development of the vehicle, politics intervened. Generaloberst von Fritsch was forced out of his position and Manstein left Army High Command. Von Fritsch was replaced by von Brauchitsch, and the program was reduced in scope. Other vested interests ranged against the plan included General Guderian—jealous that the *Panzerwaffe* might lose production—and some of the more antiquated artillery officers.

Nevertheless, in October 1937 a battery was set up at the Artillerie-Lehr-Regiment, Jüterbog. Tests went well but slowly until war intervened. The Polish campaign emphasized the need for exactly the infantry support that the vehicle—at this stage still known by the less-than-pithy title 7.5 cm Geschütz L/24 für Sturmartillerie (Selbstfahrlafette)—would provide and immediately progress was made. Daimler-Benz received an order for 30 on October 13, 1939. These were delivered between January and June 1940—with assistance from

Heinz Guderian also played an important role in the *Sturmgeschütz* story, particularly after he became *Generalinspekteur der Panzertruppen*. He felt that production of tanks should have taken preference to StuGs. (NAC)

Sturmgeschütze in France, 1940

Sturmgeschütz-Batterie 640 was employed as Infanterie-Regiment Großdeutschland's support company and would later become its 16. Sturmartillerie-Kompanie. It fought through the campaign in the West first as part of Guderian's XIX. Armeekorps and later Panzergruppe Kleist. Reorganized after the fall of France, it next took part in the invasion of Yugoslavia where it helped take Belgrade. *Die Woche*, a German weekly magazine of the time, published an article about the exploits of 16. Sturmbatterie, Infanterie-Regiment Großdeutschland. It was reproduced in English in 1941 with comments by an American observer.

> Conversations with German military personnel and the context of other articles published in German military periodicals confirm the conclusion that this assault artillery gave important and timely assistance to the leading infantry elements on many occasions ... Since this weapon is completely armored, it conforms to the commonly accepted definition of a tank. According to published accounts, this weapon, during combat, moved forward from cover to cover, keeping generally abreast of the regimental reserve. When the advance of the leading foot elements was checked by resistance beyond the capabilities of the infantry weapons immediately at hand, the armored assault artillery was ordered forward along with other heavy infantry weapons and sometimes the regimental infantry reserve. When going into action, armored assault artillery vehicles sought suitable covered positions in the front line, from which they delivered direct fire upon observed targets. It is not believed that they ever preceded and cleared the way for the foot elements. Consequently, these weapons, as employed, are not comparable to accompanying tanks.

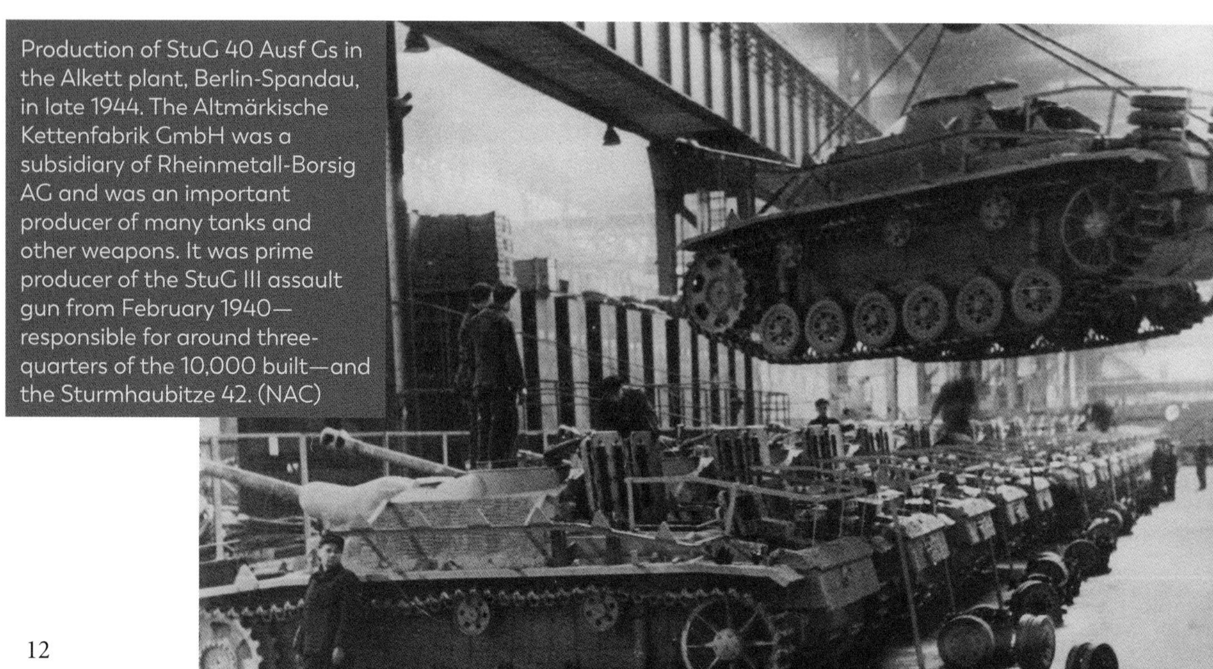

Production of StuG 40 Ausf Gs in the Alkett plant, Berlin-Spandau, in late 1944. The Altmärkische Kettenfabrik GmbH was a subsidiary of Rheinmetall-Borsig AG and was an important producer of many tanks and other weapons. It was prime producer of the StuG III assault gun from February 1940—responsible for around three-quarters of the 10,000 built—and the Sturmhaubitze 42. (NAC)

several other companies. By the time of the French campaign, which opened on May 10, 1940, four independent batteries (640, 659, 660, and 665) saw action with what became known from March 28, 1940, as the Sturmgeschütz (it only became the StuG III with the arrival of the StuG IV). Two others, Batterien 666 and 667, were a few weeks too late to take part in the fighting and instead were earmarked for *Unternehmen Seelöwe* (the planned invasion of Britain), training for this amphibious operation in Ostend and Dunkirk. At this stage each battery had six assault guns in three *Züge* (platoons) of two vehicles.

The success of the *Sturmgeschütz* units in France led to the formation of more and bigger units: the first *Abteilung* was set up in late summer 1940. StuG-Abt 184 had 18 assault guns in three batteries and was quickly followed into service by StuG-Abt 185, 190, and 191, the latter two going on to serve in the Balkan campaign where 191 supported 72. Infanterie-Division in the battles for the Greek Metaxas Line. StuG-Abt 191 later became known as the Buffalo Brigade after its unit emblem.

As with Großdeutschland, another elite unit received a *Sturmgeschütz* battery in summer 1940: the first SS *Sturmgeschütz* battery became part of LSSAH's Abteilung "Schönberger" in its August reorganization. At around the same time, a 3. (sPzJg) Kompanie equipped with Panzerjäger Is (4.7 cm Czech guns on PzKpfw I chassis) also joined the unit. As with the German Army personnel, the SS *Sturmgeschütz* crews went to the Artillerieschule Jüterbog for the formation of the battery.

North African Interlude

Between February 1941 and May 1943, German and Italian forces fought the British and, latterly, the Americans along the North African coast from Egypt to Morocco. The seesaw battles led to the creation of many myths—from the Desert Fox to the Desert Rats—but also proved a harsh environment for tracked vehicles. The heat, the abrasive sand, and the paucity of supplies all contributed to the problems. Under-resourced, their resupplies harried by Allied aircraft and naval assets, the German and Italian troops eventually surrendered in Tunisia with at least 250,000 soldiers becoming PoWs. Very few assault guns saw action in the desert. 5./Sonderverband 288 had a *Zug* of three Ausf Cs and Ds specially modified for the heat and sand. Arriving in theater in time to fight in the Gazala battles of November 1941, Sonderverband 288 became Panzergrenadier-Regiment (mot) Afrika in 90. leichte Division and fought against

It's not always hot in the desert as this well-known image of a Panzerjäger I in North Africa shows. Its four-man crew are muffled in greatcoats although the faded caps tell a different story! The 4.7 cm PaK (t) auf PzKpfw I Ausf B ohne Turm Panzerjäger I was the first in a line of *Panzerjäger* that carried through to the massive 12.8 cm-armed Jagdtiger. This Panzerjäger I is of 2./PzJg-Abt 605 which was disbanded on February 20, 1943 after heavy losses. Note the roof canvas—important for a gundeck open to the elements—and the radio aerial at back left. The vehicles started off with an Fu 2 receiver and a radio antenna at the driver's right but later vehicles were equipped with an FuG A receiver and a transmitter with the antenna moved to the position seen here. (GF Collection)

the Americans at Kasserine. It surrendered in Tunisia May 12, 1943. StuG-Brigade 242's 1. Batterie (six Ausf F/8s) was attached to 10. Panzer-Division's Panzer-Artillerie-Regiment as its 13. Batterie. Only four of the StuGs reached Africa, and it was renamed StuG-Batterie 90 at the end of April 1943. All the StuGs were lost in the fighting.

The German forces in Africa received a few *Panzerjäger* units. The first was PzJg-Abt 605, which arrived in North Africa in mid-March 1941. It had 27 Panzerjäger Is. It fought as part of Sperrverband Libyen, the first blocking force sent to the desert as part of *Unternehmen Sonnenblume*, before becoming part of 5. leichte Division and subsequently 90. leichte Division. The *Abteilung* lost Panzerjäger Is regularly (13 during British Operation *Crusader* in late November–December 1941) but received replacements and in May 1942, nine SdKfz 6/3s (a Soviet 76 mm M1936 antitank gun on a halftrack) arrived. These went into the 3. Kompanie. Attached to 90. leichte, at Gazala in late May–June of that year the *Abteilung* had four *Kompanien*—three of Panzerjäger Is of which there were 17, and one of SdKfz 6/3s. PzJg-Abt 605 received three more replacement Panzerjäger Is but could only muster 11 of them and two SdKfz 6/3s at El Alamein (September–October 1942). The unit was disbanded in late February 1943, and its remaining vehicles were passed to PzJg-Abt 190. All the Panzerjäger Is and SdKfz 6/3s were lost in Africa.

Like so many armored vehicles, the Panzerjäger I was challenged automotively—both engine and suspension—by the African conditions, although its gun and large ammunition supply were not criticized. Thomas Anderson quotes a report by Major de Bouche in August 1942 that found "troops emphasize the excellent accuracy of the gun … [but] the running gear is unreliable … The Maybach engine lacks power and easily overheats."

The largest number of tracked *Panzerjäger* to fight in the desert were Marder IIIs. At least 66 of the Ausf Ms arrived in Africa between May and November 1942. They were allocated to 15. Panzer-Division's PzJg-Abt 33 and 21. Panzer-Division's PzJg-Abt 39. The

The Marder III was based on the Czech PzKpfw 38 chassis. There were three types: Ausf G, H, and M. In November 1943 the British School of Tank Technology produced a report on the Ausf G mounting a Soviet 7.62 cm PaK 36(r), calling it "an interesting conversion particularly in view of the minimum of work involved in the change over … considerably simplified by the bolted construction of the parent vehicle. In short, the removal of the turret, superstructure top plate and engine access hatches complete the disassembly and the mounting of the gun turntable and fitting of the modified access hatches could be accomplished very speedily. The gun shields are crudely constructed and are of 10–15 mm. plate. They are open at the top and rear … The protection thus afforded is little better than would be found on a field piece … The vehicle is vulnerable from side or rear attack." The interior shows the seats of commander/gunner and loader that aren't on the traversing turntable and so are exposed when the gun is traversed. (NARA via Digital Archive)

StuG Crew Titles

From the start the *Sturmgeschütze* came under the wing of the artillery: their *Waffenfarbe* was *hochrot* (bright red) rather than the *rosa* (pink) of the *Panzer-Divisionen*. This meant different terminology as compared with the *Panzertruppen*. The organization of the *Sturmartillerie* was in *Batterien*—batteries—rather than *Kompanien*—companies. At the head of the *Batterie* was the *Batteriechef*. These *Batterien* were initially grouped together into *Abteilungen*—battalions—although later in the war they became *Brigaden*. The precise number of vehicles in a *Batterie/Abteilung/Brigade* changed during the war and is discussed in the chapter "The Vehicles." *Sturmgeschütz* crew titles were also different:

StuG title	English	PzKpfw version
Geschützführer	commander	*Panzerführer*
Richtkanonier	gunner	*Richtschütze*
Ladekanonier	loader	*Ladeschütze*
Sturmgeschützfahrer	driver	*Panzerfahrer*

gun—a conversion of the Soviet F-22 designated in German service the 7.62 cm PaK 36(r), whether bored out to receive German ammunition or not—proved extremely effective but crews bemoaned the high profile of both the SdKfz 6/3 and Marder. Additionally, some Ausf H Marder IIIs—nobody is quite sure how many—also made it to Tunisia where they ended up with 2./PzJg-Abt 39. Some sources quote over 100 Marders of both types in total in Africa. Those of PzJg-Abt 39 fought until the Axis surrender in Tunisia.

After the *Torch* landings in late 1942, 10. Panzer-Division was sent to Africa as reinforcements—although many of its vehicles never reached their destination (some 30 AFVs were lost in ships sunk by Allied attacks). On its strength were some Marder IIIs which were lost in the general surrender.

SP guns also served with German troops in Africa. Two *schwere Infanteriegeschütze-Kompanie* (sIG Kp [mot S]), 707. and 708., were created in autumn 1941 and were issued with six each of the 15 cm sIG 33 auf Fahrgestell Panzerkampfwagen II (Sf). They were allocated to Schützen-Regimenten 155 and 200 respectively, part of 90. leichte Division, arriving in Africa by April 1942. All had been lost by early December 1942, the chassis being "underpowered and liable to mechanical breakdown."

Thirty 15 cm sFH 13/1 (Sf) auf GW Lorraine Schlepper (f)s were built by Alkett specially for use in the desert, but only 23 reached Africa—the missing seven having been in ships sunk in transit. They were parceled out to 15. and 21. Panzer- and 90. leichte Divisionen and saw action at the end of the first battle of El Alamein on August 30, 1942, during which three of the 15. Panzer-Division vehicles were lost. All the others were lost during the second battle at El Alamein.

Unternehmen Barbarossa

Barbarossa started with more new *StuG-Abteilungen* formed: 192, 201, 203, 210, 226, 600, and 667, making 11 *Abteilungen* each with 21 StuGs. There were also several independent batteries. Total StuG stock at the beginning of May 1940 had been 23; a year later the number had increased to 377. The 259 vehicles that began the attack on the Soviet Union (figures here and in following lines from *Enduring the Whirlwind*) proved their worth as the German forces plunged deep into Soviet territory. The battles, however, weren't all one-sided. By the end of September, 52 *Sturmgeschütze* had been destroyed; by the end of December that figure had gone up to 104. However, production had begun to improve. From the Ausf B onward, Alkett took over as the main StuG producer and 250 Bs, 100 Cs, and the first Es—eventually nearly 300 would be delivered—helped cover the losses. It was nowhere near Manstein's original plan of a StuG unit with every infantry division, but by the time of *Fall Blau* in mid-1942, the Ostheer had 399 StuGs.

AFVs Ready for Action, July 1941–January 1943

	Jul 1, '41	Dec 1, '41	Mar 1, '42	Jul 1, '42	Jan 1, '43
PzKpfw	4,278	4,084	2,468	3,471	4,364
StuG	416	598	625	780	1,155
PaK/Sfl	–	–	–	306	1,124
Total	4,694	4,682	3,093	4,557	6,643

Total strength of the *Sturmgeschütze* increased throughout 1942: by January 1, 1943 there were 1,155 ready for action, the majority on the Eastern Front; that figure rose to 1,422 assault guns in 26 assault gun divisions and two independent batteries by June 1, 1943. They had been joined from mid-1942 by a range of tracked self-propelled artillery and antitank guns that made use of captured chassis: there were 306 of these ready for action on July 1, 1942, and 1,124 on January 1, 1943.

From the opening of *Barbarossa*, the German Army had been shocked by the Soviet heavy tanks and the T-34. Their antitank weapons had proved less than capable—particularly the 3.7 cm "Doorknocker" whose rounds simply advertised the *Panzerjägers'*

Antitank Gun on *Selbstfahrlafette* (Sfl–SP Chassis)

Type	Principal Weapon	Introduced
Marder II (SdKfz 132) on PzKpfw II	7.62 cm PaK 36 or 36(r)	Mar '42
Panzerjäger 38(t)/Marder III (SdKfz 138) on PzKpfw 38(t)	7.62 cm PaK 36 or 36(r)	May '42
Marder I (SdKfz 135) on Lorraine 37L Schlepper	PaK 40, 7.5 cm	July '42
Marder II (SdKfz 131) on PzKpfw II	PaK 40, 7.5 cm	July '42
Hornisse/Nashorn (SdKfz 165) on PzKpfw III/IV	8.8 cm PaK 43/41, L/71	Feb '43
Panzerjäger 38(t)/Marder 38(t)/ Marder III (SdKfz 139) on PzKpfw 38(t)	PaK 40, 7.5 cm	May '43

Panzerjäger

Panzerjäger I
4.7 cm PaK 36(t) on PzKpfw I

Panzerjäger I
4.7 cm PaK 36(t) on PzKpfw 35R

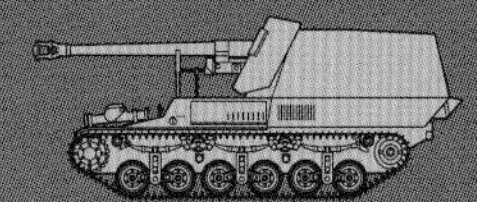
Marder I PaK 40 on PzKpfw 37L

Marder II PaK 36R on PzKpfw II

Marder III PaK 36R on PzKpfw 38

Nashorn/Hornisse

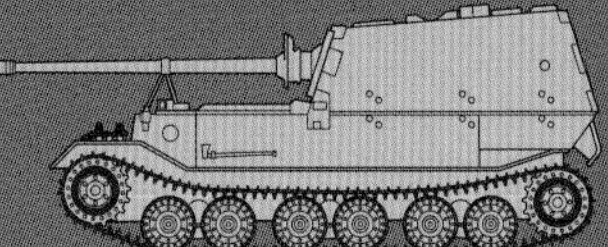
Ferdinand/Elefant

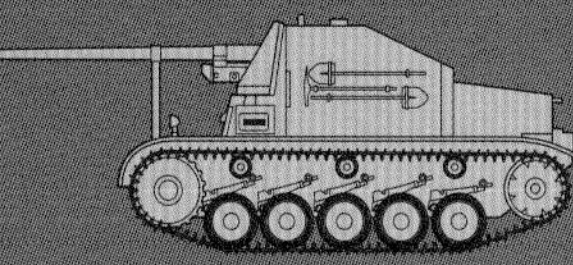
Marder II Pak 40 on PzKpfw II

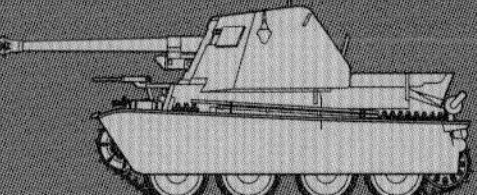
Marder III
Pak 40 on PzKpfw 38 hinten

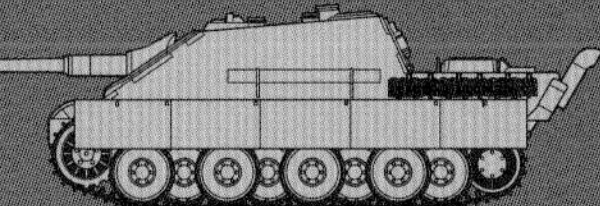
Jagdpanther

Jagdpanzer IV

Marder I PaK 40 on PzKpfw 39F

Marder II PaK 40 on PzKpfw 38 mitte

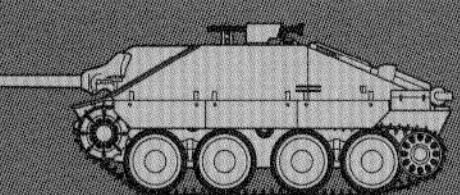
Jagdpanzer 38 (Hetzer)

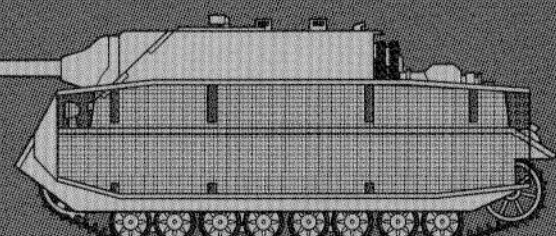
Jagdpanzer IV/70(A)

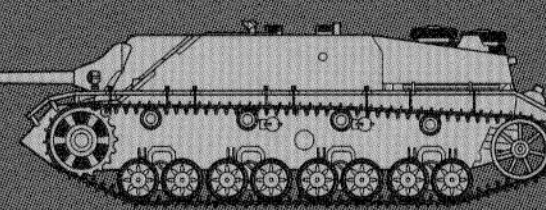
Jagdpanzer IV/70(V)

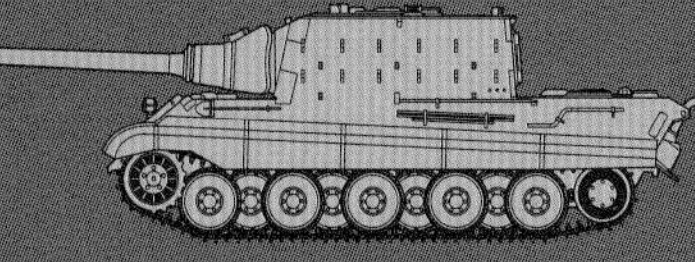
Jagdtiger

As with SP artillery, the development of the *Panzerjäger* was initially dependent on captured equipment: Czech and Soviet guns, with French, Czech, and British AFVs as chassis. The most successful of the wartime *Panzerjäger* proved to be the *Sturmgeschütz* itself. This artwork shows the development, in rough order of date of introduction into service.

Guderian's View of the Sturmgeschütz

While Guderian pragmatically pushed for the StuG to be taken into the *Panzerwaffe*, he did so reluctantly. His views were that a turreted tank was always better than a casemated assault gun for the very simple and obvious reason that the *Sturmgeschütz* only had a small amount of traverse (24° compared to 360°) and was vulnerable to attacks from the flanks and rear. Even with a close-defense weapon, lack of decent all-round vision defines the *Sturmgeschütz* as an infantry support weapon that requires an infantry escort. *Sturmgeschütze* may have lower losses than tanks, but that's because (a) they tend to have thicker frontal armor, (b) they are more closely supported by infantry, and (c) they are not the spearhead of the attack. Tanks are and their main advantages are that they can be used in attack without infantry support. A tank can be a substitute for a *Sturmgeschütz*, but a *Sturmgeschütz* cannot be the substitute for a tank. This is why he pushed so strongly for the continued manufacturing of the PzKpfw IV.

presence and did little damage to their opponents. They needed effective tank killers, and as a hurried interim measure, a range of modified chassis—such as the Marder II and III, of which there were nearly 300 available mid-1942—joined the Ostheer's inventory. Many of these weapons were constructed by Baukommando Becker outside Paris in collaboration with Alkett. Making use of French chassis such as the Lorraine 37L Schlepper, Becker was able to construct interim-measure vehicles that went to help Panzerarmee Afrika and on the Eastern Front. These vehicles often lacked strong armor and regularly suffered from automotive issues, but they were armed with effective weapons—often captured Soviet pieces—and they helped bridge a sizable manufacturing gap.

Additionally, by this time the *Sturmgeschütze* were no longer just tasked with infantry support. They also had become highly successful tank killers. Their low silhouette made them perfect for ambushing Soviet armor and from the Ausf F onward the stubby StuK 37 L/24 main armament was replaced by first the StuK 40 L/43 and then the L/48. These "*Langrohren*" (StuGs armed with long-barreled guns) were cheaper to manufacture than the increasingly complicated and expensive tanks and *Panzerjäger*. By mid-1942 185 Ausf F and F/8 had come off the production lines. The StuG 40 Ausf G entered production in December 1942: by the end of the war 7,893 had been produced by Alkett and MIAG. The most manufactured of all StuG *Ausführungen*, many went for use by *Panzer-Divisionen* in roles for which the StuG hadn't been designed but at which it proved to be effective—so much so that production of the PzKpfw IV was questioned. Should it be replaced by StuGs?

1943 opened with a catastrophe for the German war effort. Defeat of the German and Italian forces at the second battle of El Alamein (October 23–November 11, 1942) and then the successful Allied landings on the coast of Africa in November 1942 had been bad enough but the destruction and surrender of 6. Armee at Stalingrad at the end of January 1943 and the associated loss of equipment and men was even worse. Müller-Hillebrand put the losses from the associated combat January to April 1943 as 2,945 tanks, 461 *Sturmgeschütze*, and 426 *Panzerjäger*. Abteilungen 177, 190, 243, 244, and 245 were the *Abteilungen* involved at Stalingrad.

One result of this debacle was the return from the wilderness of Heinz Guderian who became *Generalinspekteur der Panzertruppen*—Inspector General of Armored Troops. Hitler signed off a wide-ranging portfolio of duties and powers for Guderian but, crucially, this did not include control of the *Sturmgeschütze*—although in his postwar autobiography *Panzer Leader* Guderian suggested that this was a result of a "trick" that had been played "on me, or rather not on me personally but on the antitank defenses of the Army and therefore on the Army as a whole." In a subsequent conference on March 9, he proposed:

(a) more use should be made of the StuGs: "I believe that it is essential that each month one tank battalion be equipped with light assault guns and incorporated into the *Panzer-Divisionen*, and that this continue until such time as the factories are producing enough tanks to meet the full requirements of the *Panzer-Divisionen*."

(b) that antitank defense—because of the lack of suitable weapons—would devolve onto the StuGs and *Panzerjäger* SP antitank guns and that "In order to economize on personnel and material, a gradual amalgamation of the assault-gun battalions and the antitank battalions is necessary."

(c) that the new heavier antitank weapons—such as Ferdinand/Elefant and Hornisse/Nashorn—should only be committed "on the major battle fronts and for special tasks."

(d) that the artillery units of armored and motorized divisions should receive adequate numbers of SP guncarriages.

As a result of the conference, a Führer decree of March 13, 1943 decided that from May 1943, every month 100 newly produced StuG IIIs were to go to the armored troops. Initially they were used to reequip the reformed armored regiments of the divisions destroyed in Stalingrad. While it was intended that some armored divisions should be completely equipped with StuGs, mixed formations—each with two tank and two StuG companies—were more often the case. The StuGs certainly proved their worth as tank destroyers; although the actual figures are difficult to come by, there's plenty of anecdotal evidence. In the fighting around Kharkov in early 1943, Großdeutschland's StuG units claimed 44 T-34s; their Tigers only 30. Around Leningrad, StuG-Abteilung 226 claimed 221 Soviet tanks for a loss of 13 of their 41 vehicles. In total the 11 *Abteilungen* fighting in August 1943 claimed 423 confirmed kills for the loss of only eight of their own.

Propaganda postcard using an image of a StuG from the *Kriegsopfer-Wandkalender der Nationsozialistischen Kriegsopferversorgung* (War Donation Wall Calendar from the NS War Aid) organization. (RCT)

Further change came on March 19, 1943. Guderian remembers in *Panzer Leader* a demonstration before Hitler at Rugenwalde where they watched the railway gun *Gustav*, the Ferdinand heavy *Panzerjäger*, and a PzKpfw IV equipped with *Schürzen* armored aprons—"sheets of armor plating which were hung loose about the flanks and rear end of the PzKpfw III, the PzKpfw IV and the StuGs; they were intended to deflect or nullify the effect of the Russian infantry's antitank weapons, which could otherwise penetrate the relatively thin, vertical body-armor of those types of vehicle. This innovation was to prove useful." That was more than he could say for the Ferdinand which he decried for lack of defensive armament which meant it was "valueless for fighting at close range. This was its great weakness." He went on to admit, "I had to find some use for it, even though I could not, on tactical grounds, share Hitler's enthusiasm for this product of his beloved Porsche."

Strategically, the German war position had altered in late 1942/early 1943 and things went from bad to worse. May 1943 saw the surrender of the Axis forces in North Africa. Guderian suggests that he tried at the start of April to arrange for the "many superfluous tank crews—particularly the irreplaceable commanders and technicians with years of experience behind them—be now flown out [of Africa]." This was refused and the chance to reform/rehabilitate units was lost. The hammer blows kept falling in 1943. In July the offensive at Kursk failed although the first two *Abteilungen* of Ferdinands—653 and 654—performed rather better than Guderian had expected, proving to have devastating firepower with over 500 Soviet tanks claimed against 39 losses. However, its awful running gear meant that mine damage often led to losses as the vehicles were too heavy to recover and were subsequently destroyed by their crew or the Soviets. Finally, to compound the annus horribilis, September 1943 saw the Allied landings in Italy.

On the defensive, the German Army had to fall back on improvisation because tank manufacturing just could not reach the needed numbers and lack of spare parts reached crisis levels. The first half of 1943 saw the phasing out of the PzKpfw III, and the production put over to the building of StuGs. Guderian wrote, "The production figure ... was to reach 220 per month by June 1943, of which 24 were to be armed with light field howitzers. This gun, with its low muzzle velocity and its very high trajectory, was undoubtedly well suited to the requirements of the infantry, but its production resulted in a fresh weakening of our defensive power against hostile tanks." When the Alkett works in Berlin was put out of action through Allied bombing, production of the StuG IV—rather than continued production of PzKpfw IVs—was mooted by Krupp. This was vehemently opposed by Guderian who argued that turreted tanks were essential and that to reach anywhere like the number required meant production of the PzKpfw IV had to be continued. After long arguments, Guderian did secure the continuation of the PzKpfw IV, but Hitler decided that once the monthly figure of 330 had been reached, further chassis should be used for turretless vehicles.

There's no doubt that Guderian's views, as a tank man, were strongly held and, all things being equal, correct: turreted vehicles were preferable to those with fixed guns. But with Allied bombing beginning to play a significant role, assault guns and *Panzerjäger* were easier, cheaper, and less time-consuming to produce than turreted tanks, and that is the main reason why German factories built them in large numbers.

The second half of 1943 and early 1944 saw the introduction of a variety of important—and often expensive—tracked weapons that, with hindsight, highlight the drawbacks of the German production system. As an example, rushed into combat at Kursk (with sPzJg-

Combat-ready Cost Comparisons

from tanks-encyclopedia.com

PzKpfw I	40,000 RM	PzKpfw IV Ausf F2	115,962 RM
PzKpfw II Ausf B	52,640 RM	Panther	150,000 RM
PzKpfw III Ausf M	103,163 RM	Tiger I	300,000 RM
StuG III Ausf G	82,500 RM	Tiger II	321,500 RM

Abt 560) before being fully tested, the Hornisse (renamed Nashorn in 1944) suffered from severe engine overheating, was difficult to camouflage because of its height, gave very little protection to its crew (open at top and back and with thin armor) but had an 8.8 cm gun that enabled the user to knock out any Allied tank from long range. In 1945, a Nashorn claimed one of the few T26E3 kills of the war, knocking out the Pershing at a range of 500 m.

Another example of a good gun mounted on the wrong chassis, the Jagdpanzer IV became known as "Guderian's *Ente*" (duck). Its low height could make firing difficult over undulating ground, although it was excellent for concealment. The Jagdpanzer IV had been designed with the Soviet tanks of 1941–42 in mind: against them, it performed well. However, against the improved Soviet vehicles of 1943–44, it was less competitive—even in its L/70 long-barreled version—particularly when set against the efforts of the StuG III and the Jagdpanther. Only 300 were produced of the latter, more powerful in every way than the Jagdpanzer IV. Even with the Panther's automotive issues, the Jagdpanther was probably the best tank destroyer of the war.

The little and large *Panzerjäger* of spring 1944 were the enormous Jagdtiger, with its 12.8 cm main gun, and the diminutive Jagdpanzer 38(t) based on the PzKpfw 38(t) chassis that had already seen so much use. Today we know it as the Hetzer and it was an excellent small tank destroyer whose only significant drawbacks were the poor all-round visibility its crew had when buttoned up, and the cramped space inside, exacerbated by the fact that the gun was off-center and took up most of the right-hand side of the vehicle. Over 2,000 of the

Panzerjäger Entering Service, 1943–44

Type	Principal Weapon	Introduced
Hornisse/Nashorn	PaK 43/3, 8.8 cm L/71	Feb–May '43 (sPzJg-Abt 525, 560, 655)
Ferdinand/Elefant	PaK 43/2, 8.8 cm L/71	Apr–May '43 (sPzJg-Abt 653, 654)
Jagdpanther	PaK 43/3, 8.8 cm L/71	Dec '43 (arrives Mielau training facility in France in Mar '44)
Jagdpanzer IV	PaK 39, 7.5 cm L/48	Spring '44
Jagdpanzer 38(t)	PaK 39, 7.5 cm L/48	Jun '44 arrives in *Panzerjäger* schools
Jagdtiger	PaK 80, 12.8 cm L/55	Late '44

Jagdpanzer 38s were built—rather more than of the behemoth built on the Tiger II chassis. Only around 70 Jagdtigers were constructed, and they appeared too late in the war to have any significant effect. Underpowered, with crews that were not as well trained as they ought to have been, more of the Jagdtigers were lost to destruction following breakdowns than enemy action.

Panzerartillerie

In the early years of the war, the function of mobile artillery for the *Panzerwaffe* was supplied by a range of improvised vehicles, such as the Sturmpanzer I and those sent to North Africa (see p. 13). Others were grafted onto the already much-traveled chassis of the PzKpfw II (the Wespe) and Pzkpfw 38(t) (the Grille). The first dedicated mobile SPG produced by German industry was the Hummel on the same chassis as the Hornisse—the Geschützwagen III/IV (Sf) designed by Alkett. The Panzerhaubitze Hummel sported a 15 cm sFH 18/1 and entered service at Kursk. It proved to be an efficient weapons system, popular with its crews. Its only drawback was that it could carry very little ammunition and needed an ammunition carrier (a Hummel without the gun) to accompany it. Manufacture of the Hummel ended when the Deutsche Eisenwerke Duisberg factory was destroyed by bombing on March 9, 1945, with 250 Hummels still on the production line.

As mentioned, other significant SP guns to arrive in mid-1943 were the Wespe and the Grille. The Grille SPG performed well enough that in December 1943 production was extended and over 350 were built. The same was true of the Wespe, 676 of which were built from February 1943 to June 1944 along with over 150 ammunition carriers. It first saw action at Kursk. However large its production run, it wasn't free from problems: there was little crew protection, it was relatively unstable cross-country, it had final drive and running gear issues, and it did not have a recoil spade which exacerbated this problem.

There were other, larger, weapons systems built to provide infantry support, particularly in builtup areas, as the StuGs became more heavily used as *Panzerjäger*: the Sturmhaubitze version of the StuG III, the Sturmpanzer IV (often called the *Brummbär* by the Allies) that entered service at Kursk in mid-1943 with Sturmpanzer-Abteilung 216, and the Sturmmörserwagen 606/4 mit 38 cm RW 61—commonly shortened to Sturmtiger. The latter two were produced in small numbers, 306 and 18 respectively, and came under the *Panzerwaffe* rather than the *Artillerie*.

The Battle of Normandy

With invasion in the West imminent, the Germans bulked up their armor in France. By June 10, the figures had changed and the percentage of armor in the East and West had, for the moment, swung toward the West. There were more tanks awaiting the Allies in Normandy than there were in the East. There were, however, fewer *Sturmgeschütze* and *Panzerjäger* in the West. From June onward, new AFVs were kept in Germany where they were used to create Hitler's organizational brainchild, the short-lived *Panzer-Brigaden*. These took up much of the year's new tank production and were designed to be used to plug defensive gaps in the East. Some had to be used in the West in September—such as Pz-Bde 107 that that saw action in Holland during Operation *Market Garden* and Pz-Bde 111 and 113 at Arracourt.

New equipment was also rushed to Normandy. Originally a StuG III replacement, the Jagdpanzer IV was developed on the Pzkpfw IV chassis, and it was planned to use it to equip *Panzerjäger-Abteilungen* in *Panzer-* and *Panzergrenadier-Divisionen*. They had just started to come in—Panzer Lehr's Panzerjäger-Lehr-Abteilung 130 being the first to receive the vehicle on June 1—before D-Day. Other units to be equipped were 2., 116., and 12. SS-Panzer-Divisionen, each receiving 21 vehicles, while the Panzer-Lehr and 17. Panzergrenadier-Divisionen had 31, the latter's arriving in August. In Italy, the Hermann Göring Panzer-Division and 3. and 15. Panzergrenadier-Divisionen received a total of 83, of which number fewer than 10 survived the year. On the Eastern Front there were 300 left by the end of 1944.

The Jagdpanther arrived in dribs and drabs during June, equipping 654. schwere Panzerjäger-Abteilung which used it successfully in a well-known engagement with the Scots Guards near Saint-Martin-du-Bois during Operation *Bluecoat*. The unit retreated through Falaise and was fully up to strength (45 Jagdpanthers) by November 15.

Also sent to Normandy was Sturmpanzer-Abteilung 217. It took some time to reach the area from its training grounds at Grafenwöhr, and it arrived piecemeal, the first elements—a company, probably 2. Kompanie—arrived on July 21 and was subordinated to 21. Panzer.

Operation *Bagration*

On the Eastern Front, just over two weeks after D-Day, the Red Army launched the operation that swept away Heeresgruppe Mitte and liberated what was left of the Nazi-controlled Soviet Union. By this time the armored strength in the East comprised:

- *Panzer-* and *Panzergrenadier-Divisionen*: 1,289 PzKpfw IV/Panther/Tiger tanks (of which 334 were in repair), 178 StuGs (of which 30 in repair) (Figures from S. Zaloga)
- StuG units (over 32 *Abteilungen/Brigaden*): 925 (215 in repair) StuGs and StuHs (Figures from S. Zaloga)
- *Infanterie-Divisionen Panzerjäger* units: c. 375 all told (mainly Panzerjäger 38s, Marders, and StuGs; some Nashorns, e.g., 78. Sturmdivision)

Unfortunately for Heeresgruppe Mitte, the OKH expected the Soviets to attack in the South and had deployed most of their armored strength there. Ranged against the c. 500 tanks and

German 6. Armee advances on Stalingrad, August 1942. Leading the file of StuGs is an Ausf F/8 armed with a 7.5 cm main gun. The Ausf F and F/8 were the first StuGs to use the longer main gun, something that promoted its role as a *Panzerjäger*. (tormentor4555PDM/WikiCommons/1.0 DEED)

Self-propelled Guns

The battles in Poland in 1939 made it clear that the German Army needed artillery that could keep pace with the advance. During the war the SP guns developed from the ramshackle Panzerjäger I that married PzKpfw I chassis with a Czech 4.7 cm gun to the enormous Sturmtiger armed with a huge 38 cm rocket-propelled mortar.

Sturmpanzer I Bison

10.5 cm leFH 16 on Mk VI

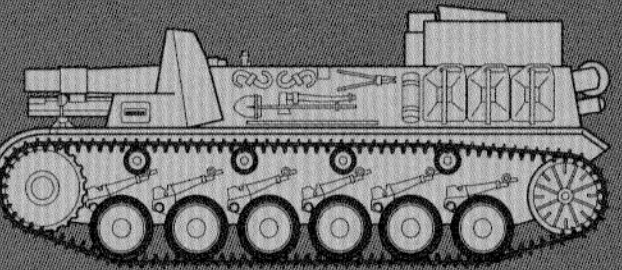

sIG 33 auf Fahrgestell PzKpfw II (Sf) (Sturmpanzer II)

Sturm-Infanteriegeschütz 33B (Sturmpanzer III)

Grille Ausf H

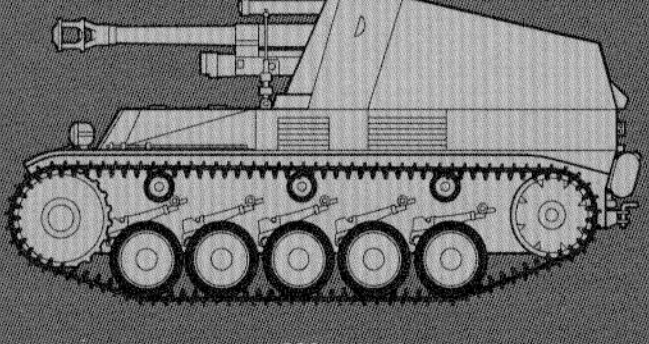

Wespe

Sturmpanzer IV

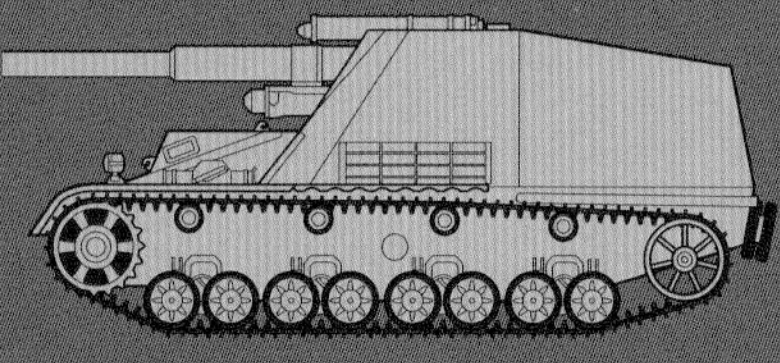

Hummel

Grille Ausf K

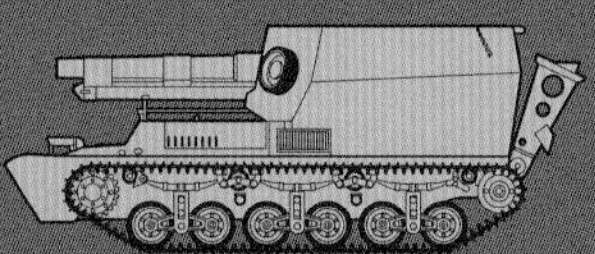

Becker sFH13/1 on 37L

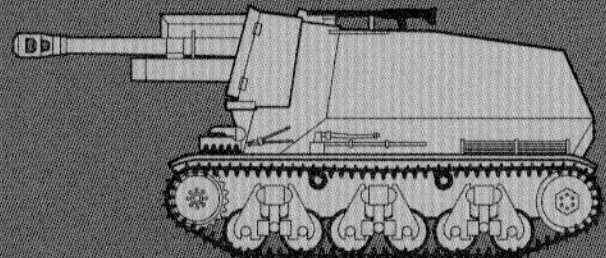

Becker le FH18 on 39H

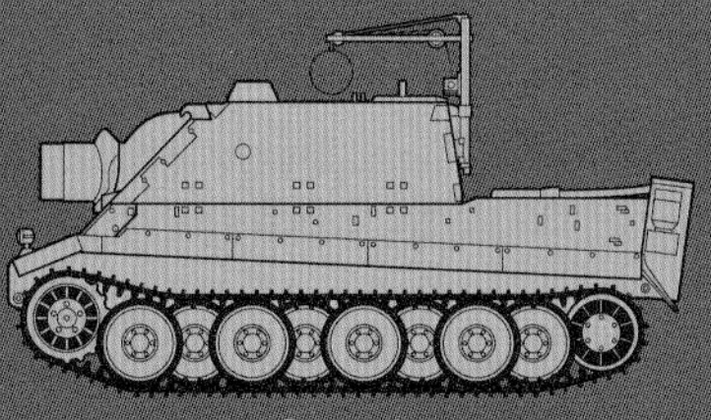

Sturmtiger

SP and Heavy Assault Guns from Late 1942

Type	Principal Weapon	Date Introduced
Sturmhaubitze 42 (SdKfz 142/2) on StuG III	10.5 cm StuH 42 L/28	Late '42
Grille (SdKfz 138/1) on PzKpfw 38(t)	15 cm sIG 33/1 (Ausf H) and /2 (Ausf K)	Spring '43
Wespe (SdKfz 124) on PzKpfw II	10.5 cm leFH 18/2	May '43
Hummel (SdKfz 124) on PzKpfw II	15 cm leFH 18/2	May '43
Sturmpanzer IV (SdKfz 166) on PzKpfw IV	15 cm StuH 43 L/12	May '43
Sturmtiger on Tiger I	38 cm RW 61 L/5.4	Aug '44

SP guns—of which the majority were StuGs—of HG Mitte were the 4,000 tanks and assault guns of four Soviet fronts (with a further 1,750 of the 1st Belorussian Front who subsequently joined in). Unsurprisingly, the Germans were unable to stem the Soviet tide, although the Red Army lost nearly 3,000 tanks in the fighting (knocked out—not all were destroyed). The attack continued to the south as part of the Lvov–Sandomierz Offensive that took the Red Army to the Vistula. In the north, HG Nord was trapped in the Kurland Peninsula where it remained for the rest of the war. As the Soviet attack ground to a halt, the German defenses held, and the focus of the fighting shifted to Romania. The German AFV losses had been serious. Zaloga quotes what he identifies as incomplete data from German sources: tanks 1,808, StuG IIIs/IVs 1,587, Marders I–III 460, and Nashorns 109, for a total of 3,964.

The Battle of the Bulge

The arrival of the Western Allies in France, the huge losses caused by Operations *Overlord* and *Bagration*, and the continuous bombardment of German industry from the air doomed the Third Reich. The only real question was how long it would take before the end came. The result of the Normandy campaign had been a complete victory for the Allies. Few of the 2,000–2,500 AFVs committed in the West crossed the Seine as they retreated through the Falaise Gap toward Germany, chased closely by the Allies. What was surprising was the fact that the German Army—badly defeated in the East and West—was able to construct a defense. Some of this was due to the Allies' logistics. Having advanced so far on both fronts they needed a period to allow maintenance and refreshment of tired units. Some of it was down to the resilience of the Wehrmacht, determined to protect their homeland. Some of it was down to the fact that German industry, despite everything, was finally hitting its stride.

German weapons' production in the last months of the war was remarkable. In July 1944 the number of available tanks reached 5,800, a wartime peak. Even after the losses on both fronts, in early 1945 the German Army still had nearly 4,000 AFVs on the Western and Eastern Fronts, and when the number of vehicles available everywhere is considered, that number doubled.

One of the new additions to the German inventory for the Normandy campaign, as mentioned earlier, the Jagdpanzer IV had not been available in the quantities hoped for. In August the longer-gunned PzKpfw IV/70 was introduced. Coinciding with Hitler's short-lived idea of smaller "*Panzer-Brigaden*," the first PzKpfw IV/70(V)s were provided to the 105. and 106. Panzer-Brigaden in August followed in September by the 107., 108., 109., 110., and the Führer-Grenadier-Brigade—but training and availability meant that it wasn't until the end of the year that the PzKpfw IV/70 saw widespread use. Indeed, for all the improved manufacturing numbers, what the Germans couldn't do was create suitably trained tank and assault-gun crews quickly enough to man the new vehicles effectively. This was to be shown up by Panzer-Brigaden 111 and 113 around Arracourt in September 1944 when undertrained and inexperienced crews in new Panthers proved no match for the battle-experienced U.S. 4th Armored Division and lost over 200 tanks and 122 *Jagdpanzer* and StuGs. The *Panzer-Brigaden*, seemingly on paper so strong in tanks and assault guns, didn't have the ancillary equipment of a *Panzer-Division* and proved ineffective.

The Jagdpanther had also begun to arrive in greater quantities. Between April and July 1944 sPzJg-Abt 654 and 559 had received full contingents of the vehicle, the former fighting in Alsace after escaping Normandy, the latter in Holland before moving to Alsace to fight with Panzer Lehr. Christian Ankerstjerne identifies the main recipients of the Jagdpanther (in lifetime figures) as: sPzJg-Abt 519: 27, sPzJg-Abt 559: 56, sPzJg-Abt 560: 39, sPzJg-Abt 654: 100, sPzJg-Abt 655: 24, Pz-Regt 130, and Pz-Lehr-Division: 49.

The Jagdpanther certainly performed well in the field, when it was running, although there weren't many units involved. Its initial problem was—as with the Panther—its final drive and its reliability. The well-known engagement with the Scots Guards near Saint-Martin-du-Bois during Operation *Bluecoat* alluded to earlier saw three Jagdpanthers of sPzJg-Abt 654 knock out 11 Churchills but the battalion was forced back and had to abandon two slightly damaged Jagdpanthers and a command Panther. By September and October, however, improvements had been made and by early November sPzJg-Abt 654 had 45 Jagdpanthers. They'd lose 18 in the month but kill 52 enemy tanks by the end of the month; after receiving 20 new vehicles, they had 44 operational, which reduced to 28 on December 30 with seven more under repair.

November saw the refitting and regeneration of the *Panzer-Divisionen* in time for the last throw of the dice in the West, which was launched on December 16, 1944, *Unternehmen Wacht am Rhein*. On December 15, 1,216 tanks and assault guns were ready for action in the West from a total of 1,695 vehicles. These included 598 StuGs (410 operational) and 503 (391) PzKpfw IVs, including PzKpfw IV/70(Vs and As), and FlakPz IVs. Also involved was

The range of German armor is well illustrated in this 1945 view of AFVs knocked out and abandoned during the battles for Budapest. From right: a PzKpfw III, a Hummel, an ammunition transporter based on the Hummel; then a Jagdpanzer 38(t), and behind it the barrel of a Grille is visible. (Vörös Hadsereg/Fortepan)

The end is nigh: StuG IVs of 2./Panzerjäger-Abteilung 34, 34. Infanterie-Division, moving into Ivrea, north of Turin to surrender to U.S. 34th Infantry Division in early May 1945. They are part of the German LXXV. Armeekorps that had fought in northern Italy 1944–45. (NARA)

sPzJg-Abt 559, returned from Alsace. It fought around Wiltz and Bastogne before being pushed back through Houffalize where it lost its last six Jagdpanthers. (It received more in April 1945; too late to do any more than retreat in front of the victorious Red Army.)

Around 1,000 tanks and assault guns were used in the Ardennes: over 500 were lost as the U.S. Army first delayed the attack's timetable, then held the attack, and finally rolled the Germans back with great losses. Remarkably, despite this, new equipment meant that on February 5, 1945, AFV strength in the West was 1,420 (810 operational).

AFV Strength at the Western Front February 5, 1945

	Strength	Ready for action
Tanks	390	190
Nashorn	12	8
StuG and Jagdpz IV	892	533
Assault tank	32	15
Jagdpanther	66	43
Jagdtiger	28	21
Total StuG/Jagdpz	1,030	620
Grand Total	1,420	810

The problem for the Germans from the August 1944 onward was that no sooner were units rebuilt than they had to be committed to the fray with new equipment and undertrained troops, where they were destroyed again. In the East, on January 5, 1945, the German defenses were based around nearly 4,000 AFVs.

AFV Strength with Field Forces on the Eastern Front, January 5, 1945

	PzKpfw units	StuG Brigaden*	PzJg Kompanien**	Total Eastern Front
Tanks (PzKpfw IV–VI)	1,292			1,292
StuG/Jagdpz	641	902	949	2,492
Total	1,933	902	949	3,784

* *StuG Brigaden* are GHQ troops for the reinforcement of infantry divisions.

** *PzJg Kompanien* are component parts of infantry divisions.

Repair Services

The reason for the number of the AFVs available for the defence of the Reich was not just production totals but the exemplary work undertaken by the repair services. German figures on losses of AFVs should always be tempered by the knowledge that most knocked-out tanks were salvaged—something their more profligate and better-equipped enemies didn't do with the same level of commitment. Müller-Hillebrand suggests that "During the latter part of the war, 95 percent of damages were repaired by the field forces, and at least 95 percent of these within the tank regiment, while only about 5 percent of the damages were repaired in repair shops in the Zone of the Interior."

Repair Services at the Front

Month	Pz II–VI	StuG	PaK Sfl	Total	Motors
Oct '43	973	652	200	1,825	143
Nov '43	911	698	195	1,804	216
Dec '43	1,294	873	224	2,391	2,831
Jan '44	2,190	1,111	938	4,239	228
Total				10,259	

Repair Services in the Zone of the Interior

Month	Pz II–VI	StuG	PaK Sfl	Total
Oct '43	62	22	45	129
Nov '43	90	19	36	145
Dec '43	57	41	30	128
Jan '44	71	91	39	201
Total				603

There was little, however, that the repair services could do in the face of the onslaught that was unleashed on January 12, 1945, when the Red Army attacked across the Vistula with forces that included 4,529 tanks and 2,513 assault guns. By February 2, they were at the Oder. After a brief delay to clear the so-called Baltic shelf, the battle for Berlin began on April 14. Two weeks later, it was all over. Hitler was dead and the Wehrmacht had surrendered.

Estonia 1943, a freestanding A-frame pulley-block gantry is used to remove a 7.5 cm PaK 40/3 L/46 gun from a Marder III. A mixed crew is involved, and the number—10 people in total—shows how heavy and unwieldy these items were. Note pulley chains and illegible name on the side. (Dutch Archives)

A StuG 40 Ausf G awaits the return of its drive wheel or a replacement. It doesn't look like a dangerous area—the crewman waiting with the vehicle seems to be enjoying the sunshine. Had things been more active the radio sets and other demountable equipment would have been loaded onto trailers and taken to safety. The German maintenance and retrieval systems functioned well during the war until AFV weights reached a level that required specialist retrieval vehicles. These were in too short a supply and led to many retrievable vehicles being destroyed by their crews. (Ian Spring/Pixpast.com)

A 10.5 cm leFH 18M L/28 gun is being lifted onto a Wespe with a Bilstein 6-tonne lift crane mounted on a Bilstein-modified, 18-tonne Famo SdKfz 9/1 halftrack. Small detail: note the hanging clipboard on the rear armor plate. (Bundesarchiv, Bild 101I-312-0968-17A)

The Soldier

Training

Sturmgeschütz Crew

The *Sturmgeschütz* from the outset fell under the aegis of the artillery arm of service—and until 1943, soldiers of all ranks were exclusively volunteers. Training started at Jüterbog Artillery School. A military site from the late 19th century when the Berlin Artillery School moved there, under Nazi control the school was expanded. In 1934 the Adolf-Hitler-Lager in Forst Zinna became the third camp on the site, now the largest military complex in Germany. The SS were the first to use it; from 1935 it was used for artillery observation units.

The center of the StuG arm started at Jüterbog in the form of 7. Batterie/Artillerie-Lehr-Regiment, then progressed to VI. Abteilung Artillerie-Lehr-Regiment, and later III./ Artillerie-Lehr-Regiment 2 (mot). It remained at Jüterbog until 1943.

At different times, the teaching staff (*Lehrstab*) was divided into sections whose names also changed:

- Lehrstab A—called the Artillerie-Waffenschule from August 26, 1939, to May 18, 1940.
- Lehrstab B—called Beobachtungsschule (Observation School) Jüterbog during the same period as above.
- Lehrstab C—from January 15, 1942, *Vermessungs- und Kartenwesen* (Surveying and Mapping).
- *Lehrstab für Offiziers-Schießlehrgänge* (officers' shooting courses)—from February 20, 1940.
- Lehrstab T (driver training)—from August 10, 1941.

Turretless training *Fahrschulpanzer* (driving-school tank), this one based on a PzKpfw II chassis, at a Wehrmacht training ground in Germany in 1940. Much driver training was undertaken by instructors of the NSKK—the Nationalsozialistisches Kraftfahrkorps or National Socialist Motor Corps. (Ian Spring/Pixpast.com)

In 1942, the Jüterbog Artillery School was split into Artillery School I in Berlin (it later moved to Meißen on April 1, 1944) and Artillery School II in Jüterbog (it moved on August 1, 1943, to Groß-Born—today's Borne Sulinowo in Poland).

The old Artillerieschule's Department D—the Army Intelligence School—had helped set up the Heeresnachrichtenschule (Army Signals School) in Halle and had moved there in 1935–36. All German AFVs carried radios and the *Sturmgeschütze* were no exception. Training for the wireless operator's role in the StuG was undertaken at Halle. There was also a *Nachrichtenlehrgang* (communications training course) at Jüterbog.

On July 15, 1943, the Sturmartillerieschule was set up by Artillery School II in the Fürst Leopold von Anhalt-Dessau Barracks at Burg near Magdeburg. It consisted of *Aufstellungsstab* teaching staff, and *Sturmartillerie-Lehr-Abt* (assault artillery training section) with three batteries. From 1944, this school was renamed the Sturmgeschützschule Burg with courses I to V and the Sturmgeschütz-Lehr-Abteilung. The staff for the formation of new StuG units (*StuG-Aufstellungsstab*) was based at the nearby Altengrabow training area.

Subordinate to Artillery School II were a number of reserve *Abteilungen*—200 at Schweinfurt (later transferred to Schieratz in Warthegau), 300 at Neisse, 400 at Hadersleben (Denmark), 500 at Posen (today's Poznań, Poland), 600 at Deutsch Eylau (today's Iława, Poland), Training Staff West at Tours, France (personnel only), and Training Staff Altengrabow (from 1943 responsible for all equipment at all new installations).

Sturmgeschützschule Burg was commanded by the then Oberst Gunter Hoffmann-Schönborn and quickly enlarged to include tactical and technical staff, weapons schools, technical innovations, and training of the Feldersatzheer, the Field Replacement Army.

As the war went on these training establishments were formed into units that fought vainly to defend the Reich. On April 10, 1945, the school at Burg was disbanded and Hoffmann-Schönborn's successor, Oberstlt Alfred Müller, formed and commanded Kampfgruppe Burg. Two weeks later it joined other units to become the Infanterie-Division Ferdinand von Schill, the last division formed in the Third Reich.

There were other important artillery schools at Thorn (Toruń, Poland): from 1942, the Artillerie-Schießschule that became Artillerieschule III, Thorn, on January 15, 1943. It moved to Suippes-Mourmelon, Châlons-en-Champagne in France two months later and was renamed Schule III für Fahnenjunker der Artillerie on April 28, 1943. Also at Thorn from 1942 was the Heeresunteroffiziersschule der Artillerie. It moved to Amberg, Bavaria in August 1944. Subordinate to the Heeresunteroffiziersschule Amberg from October 26, 1944, was the Feld-Unteroffiziersschule der Artillerie, Autun. *The German Replacement Army* (U.S. War Dept. 1944) identifies various other *Artillerieschulen* for special courses such as Barth (for rapid firing instruction), Oppeln, Neneschau near Prague, and Béziers in France.

Artillery training emphasized gunnery. The trainees learned the artillery way of doing things: fire correction—straddling and splitting, rather than re-estimating the range after a miss as gunners in the *Panzerwaffe* were taught. The artillerymen were faster at ranging in than tank crews. Every member of the crew was taught to act on their own initiative if they spotted danger. Once the *Langrohren* came in, the *Sturmgeschütz* role shifted toward antitank defense and the tactics changed to focus on ambush. The success of the antitank

Knife and Fork

It was rare to get close enough to your opponent to ensure a first time shot hit and killed him, so most shooting needed to be zeroed in. In *Panzer Gunner*, Bruno Friesen talks about techniques used by tank gunners: forking—*gabeln*—saw firing left, right, and center; knife-blade shooting—best for flat terrain—saw one short, one long, and then the hit. In artillery terms, the fork is slightly different, as explained in the U.S. Army's *FM6-40 Field Artillery Gunnery*: "Fork is the term used to express the change in elevation in mils [German = *Strich*] necessary to move the center of impact four (4) range probable errors." The range probable error is the error in range that a weapon may be expected to exceed as often as not.

When one adds into the equation the lead needed for moving targets and the general fog of war, worries about getting hit oneself, etc., it becomes obvious that coolness under fire, excellent training, and good optics are essentials. German optics were second to none and the reticles—lines and markings on the sight—were designed to help. Most showed triangles that allowed a target's width and/or height to be approximated. If the gunner knew that, he could calculate range.

The Germans used a range of gunsights for the various AFVs. The ZF (*Zielfernrohr* = telescopic sight) was a standard gunsight with a x3 magnification and 8° field of view. It equipped the 4.7 cm PaK 36(t) and the Nashorn. The Sfl ZF 1 (*Selbstfahrlafette-Zielfernrohr* = self-propelled gun telescopic sight), had a x5 magnification and 8° field of view. It equipped the Jagdpanzer 38 and IV; the Sfl ZF 1a equipped the Ferdinand/Elefant, Sturmhaubitze, and Sturmpanzer. The Sturmgeschütz started life with an Rbl F 32 (*Rundblickfernrohr* = panoramic gunsight; x4, 7°); from the Ausf C this was replaced by a Sfl ZF 1; later models such as the Ausf G used the Sfl ZF 1a. Other scopes included: the WZF 2/1 (*Winkelzielfernrohr* = angled telescopic sight, x10, 7°) used on the Jagdtiger, and ZF 1138 used on the Hetzer and other vehicles with a remote MG. The SP guns used artillery sighting methods. Both Wespe and Hummel used the Rbl F 36 on a ZE 34.

Sturmgeschütze is shown by one of the Jüterbog trainees: Michael Wittmann, of later fame with the Tigers of sSSPzAbt 101 of the LSSAH. On April 25, 1940, Wittmann transferred to an assault-gun battery at Jüterbog, where he started learning how to fight in the StuG III Ausf A. He went on to fight in StuGs on the Eastern Front and his exploits there have been frequently published—often hagiographically—many of them taking at face value the SS propaganda machine. The stories about his multiple kills with a *Sturmgeschütz* do illustrate, however, the importance of competence by driver and gunner, often acting under their own initiative. Wittmann's two best-known gunners were Karl Brüggenkamp and Alfred Günther (who also died in a Tiger in Normandy). Wittmann's success led him to SS officer training at the SS-Junkerschule in Tölz and his command of a Tiger unit.

Bruno Bork joined Sturmartillerie-Abteilung 191 in October 1940 at Jüterbog Old Camp. One of the first four *Abteilungen* set up after the fall of France, StuG-Abt 191 (the designation changed from *Sturmartillerie* to *Sturmgeschütz* in January 1941)—later known as the Buffalo Brigade—would fight with distinction until it surrendered in Austria in 1945. Its first CO was Hauptmann Günter Hoffmann-Schoenborn, who went on to command Artillerie-Lehr-Regiment 2 in 1943, Sturmgeschützschule Burg in 1943–44, and as a *Generalmajor* in 18. Volksgrenadier Division.

Formed at the Artillerie-Lehr-Regiment, the NCOs and men—all volunteers from artillery and motor vehicle units—were assigned to their batteries on arrival. Bruno Bork remembered:

> Once the authorized strength in personnel had been reached, the batteries were put together. Vehicles and equipment were fetched from the works and supply compounds, the StuGs from the Altmark track factory, Alkett in Berlin … Each battery received six StuG assault guns armed with 7.5 cm cannon, and the corresponding number of armored halftrack command [usually SdKfz 253 leichter Gepanzerter Beobachtungskraftwagen artillery observation halftracks] and ammunition vehicles. A specially designed plan had as many men under training at a time as possible. …

A shooting training facility using a StuK 37 gun mounting removed from an StuG III Ausf B and attached to a stand. Another photo of the same group shows the clear markings of StuG-Abt 189, which was set up on July 10, 1941. It went on to become Sturmgeschütz-Brigade 189 in 1944. One reason for the success of the *Sturmgeschütz-Abteilungen* was the accuracy of their shooting, a product of artillery training. (Akira Takiguchi)

> Once the formation of the Abteilung was completed, it transferred into the Adolf-Hitler-Lager where the batteries underwent battle training, the high point being the firing of live ammunition across the wide expanses of the training depot. …
>
> Shortly before Christmas 1940 exercises at Jüterbog troop depot were followed by an inspection. We felt sure that this heralded a move out. Our Abteilung Commanding Officer Hoffmann-Schoenborn was promoted to Major. Some men were given Christmas leave, those who remained spent a noisy, restless time.

On New Year's Day, Abteilung 191 was loaded onto rail transport for Romania; two months later they motored through Bulgaria. On April 6, 1942, they attacked Greece's Metaxas Line and put their training into practice.

Panzerjäger Crew

There were several *Panzerjägerschulen*, the biggest being at Truppenübungsplätze Mielau—today's Mława in Poland—and Milowitz near Prague. Other training centers of armored units and *Panzerjäger* included: Rembertow (where there was a Feld-Unteroffiziersschule der Schnellen Truppen); Putlos (for example, from August 1942 Panzerjäger-Lehr-Kp 7.5 cm or 7.62 cm [Sf] trained there); Bergen/Fallingbostel (from May 1944 there was Panzerjäger-Sturmgeschütz-Lehr-Kp [7.5 cm StuK] there which became, eventually, a Jagdpanzer 38 Kp with 9 FJD in February 1945); and Panzerjägerschule Grafenwöhr.

Nicknamed "New Berlin," the sizable Truppenübungsplatz Mielau or Northern Military Training Area (one of three in occupied Poland) was used for testing antitank and artillery weapons and housed repair facilities for tanks (including Tiger and Panther) and a military training range. The training groups at Mielau included those for the Jagdpanzer IV and 38(t)—drivers, *Panzerwarte* (mechanics), and communications. As examples, StuG-Abt 1291 was training on the StuG IV in Mielau (June–September 44); StuG-Abt 1548 also on the StuG IV June–August 1944; PzJg-Kp 1021 trained there on the Jagdpanzer 38 from October 1944 until January 1945. The men of Panzerjägerschule Mielau ended up fighting the Red Army as it reached the school.

There was a Heeresunteroffiziersschule (Panzerjäger) at Kolberg. Typical training for *Panzerjäger* recruits would cover the 7.5 cm PaK, Panzerschreck, Panzerfaust, Tellermine,

StuG III Ausf A or B used at a driving school. The main armament (a 7.5 cm StuK 37 L/24) has been removed. (World War photos)

and other explosives, and they would receive antitank close-combat training. From Kolberg they could go to a *Panzerjägerschule* such as Milowitz for further training on tracked vehicles such as the Jagdpanzer 38 which had, of course, the same 7.5 cm gun.

The training areas were used to refresh and rebuild units. An example is the Schatten-Division Milowitz that gave up two *Grenadier-Regimenter* and an *Artillerie-Bataillon* to refresh the 389. Infanterie-Division which on February 18, 1944, after the Cherkassy Pocket battles, had fewer than 2,000 men.

SS *Panzerjäger* Training

The SS had its own arms schools and specialist training programs. SS-Artillerieschule I was set up on June 1, 1942, at the Artillery Measuring School in Glau bei Trebbin (near Berlin). SS-Artillerieschule II was set up in December 1943 on the Truppenübungsplatz Böhmen at Beneschau near Prague. Waffen-SS Sturmgeschütz-Schule (Bukovan) at Janovice nad Úhlavou (Janowitz an der Angel) in Czechoslovakia on July 15, 1944 became the SS-Panzerjäger (Sturmgeschütz) Schule Janowitz. It was organized into: Kommando Stab (HQ staff); Stabs-Kompanie (HQ Company); Lehrgruppe I (Training Group I); Lehrgruppe II (Training Group II); Lehrgruppe III (T) (Training Group III [technical]); schwere Panzerjäger Lehr-Kompanie (mot Z); and Panzerjäger (Sturmgeschütz) Lehr-Kompanie.

The *Panzerjäger* allocation was StuG IVs and Jagdpanzer 38(t)s. SS NCOs (*Unterführer*) would go through the SS-Unterführerschule Lauenburg and then on to courses at Janowitz (for example, gunnery or driving courses).

The SS-Panzergrenadier Schule was at Prosetzchnitz (renamed Kienschlag in 1944) in Czechoslovakia (today's Prosečnice in the Czech Republic). New weapons and tactics were practiced there with the help of the SS-Panzergrenadier-Lehr-Regiment. Additionally, foreign officer candidates were trained there, and German SS officer aspirants were sent to Kienschlag to be assessed for suitability before being assigned to a *Junkerschule*.

New Recruits

The training of soldiers prewar was extensive, and once the war came, this meant there were sufficient troops to accommodate losses. However, *Barbarossa* changed that and as the casualty levels rose, so did the influx of new recruits. Training times began to be abbreviated. Hermann Röhm was called up in autumn 1941. On October 2 he reported in at Essling (Vienna) before being inducted into the artillery through Ludwigsburg and, after transfer to Epinal in France, s.Artillerie-Ersatz-Abteilung (mot) 61. From October 9 till December 1, 1941, he trained as a driver before being sent to Jüterbog by train and was drafted into the *Sturmartillerie* on December 8. Four days later he took over a vehicle.

Bruno Friesen was called up in early October 1942, reporting to Panzer-Ersatz-Abteilung 10 at Gross-Glienicke, Wehrkreis III, at the beginning of November. His basic training—as with every recruit—was for infantrymen and included practice on the MG 34, K98k, handguns, and grenades. It also was where many soldiers who went on to become gunners received their first lessons in gunnery in the form of "a scope-equipped .22-calibre single-shot barreled action clamped into a single traverse-and-elevation mechanism built into the front of a plywood turret supported by four sturdy legs ... Right there and then—that early in a Panzer soldier's career—his instructors could tell if he had any feeling for lead."

After two months of this, it was on to the *Fahrschule* at Lyck in East Prussia (Wehrkreis I) where he learnt to drive on a PzKpfw IA ohne Aufbau—a turretless tank—the course lasting until April 30, 1943, when he received his license. He then joined Regiment 25 and—after spending time in Italy—returned to the unit's depot at Bamberg where he received updated tank training. He remembers that much gunnery knowledge came from "battle-seasoned gunners who participated in the unofficial training, in the barracks of the replacement units, of their eventual successors in the field." For most gunners the period of apprenticeship was as a loader in action. Bruno Friesen expands:

> There were, really, no better-qualified instructors, no more extensive firing ranges and training areas, and, for that matter, no keener fellow students than those at the front lines. If a loader survived the battles and displayed the proper aptitude and attitude, that experience constituted a great step toward his becoming a gunner. … During the many hours that he spent in proximity of the gunner, his main mentor, the loader would learn quite a bit about the gunner's duties. … He would know where to find, up on the telescopic sight, the rather secluded switch for the reticle illumination. He would know how to jab the emergency impulse generator to fire the main gun after the Panzer's electrical system had failed …

Fliegende Lehrkommandos

As the war went on and the Wehrmacht was stretched thinner and thinner, casualties meant that training programs were even more abbreviated, and training units were amalgamated to allow more trained personnel to be sent to the front. As was explained in *Nachrichtenblatt der Panzertruppen*, from September 15, 1944, there was to be a shortened training period for armored troops in the reserve army—uniformly set at 12 weeks for all branches of the armed forces. Recruits were trained within eight weeks in such a way that field deployment was guaranteed from the ninth week. However, additional extended training was planned for the ninth to twelfth weeks and there was on-the-spot training by "flying training detachments."

These detachments became more and more important to ensure that tactical information—and even basic knowledge—was passed to the front. Rolf Stoves highlighted the problem in his 1985 book, discussing the poor gunnery training exposed by the arrival of newly formed III./PzRgt 204 in the Crimea from France. Reported to the OKH representative who visited to check on the unit, the result was a training detachment sent from Panzerschießschule Putlos complete with the necessary ammunition to iron out the unit's deficiencies.

In the *Nachrichtenblatt der Panzertruppen* of November 1944, a section laid out the details of how the flying training detachments could be requested for field units that either were

The monthly *Nachrichtenblatt der Panzertruppen* was sent out by the *Generalinspekteur der Panzertruppen*'s Training Department. It is headed secret and provides analysis of German weapons and tactics, successes and failures—and those of the opposition. (GF Collection)

being set up or needed refreshing. There were six areas of coverage: *Panzer*, *Panzergrenadiere* (armored and unarmored), *Panzerjäger*, *Panzer* reconnaissance, and Signals.

1. For ***Panzer*** the training detachments would be set up on a case-by-case basis, their composition according to the tasks and the level of training required, but as an example, a detachment could consist of two officers (CO/tactical instructor and a firing instructor), eight NCOs as commander instructors, four radio instructors, one weapons NCO, one master gunner, two driving instructors, two armorer instructors.

2. For ***Panzergrenadiere* (armored)** there were five available tactical training detachments; four field training detachments for heavy weapons—to train gunners, commanders, and platoon leaders of heavy weapons units (medium and heavy mortars, 7.5 cm KwK, leIG, and sIC); two special field training detachments for training on the Kfz 251/21 drilling; five driving instruction detachments that included an NCO tank driver instructor to train APC drivers in tactical offroad driving etc.

3. For ***Panzergrenadiere* (unarmored)** there were no permanent training detachments available for these units. In urgent cases, tactical and field training detachments for heavy weapons could be organized.

4. For ***Panzerjäger*** there were 15 training detachments for individual to unit training on StuG IIIs, StuG IVs, and Jagdpanzer 38(t)s. These were made up of four officers, one radio instructor (officer if possible), one weapons instructor, two driving instructors, two tank mechanic instructors, one tank radio operator, and one weapons sergeant.

5. For ***Panzer* reconnaissance** there were two training detachments with the task of supporting the reorganization and refresher training in tactics and technical matters. They were made up of instructors for armored scout and reconnaissance companies, engineers, 7.5 cm KwK, 8 cm mortars, and—in particular—driving and mechanics.

6. **Signals training detachments** There were three of these each with a CO, *Panzer/Panzergrenadiere/Panzerjäger/Panzer* reconnaissance signals officers and radio communication instructors.

All the listed training units had to be requested from the *Generalinspekteur der Panzertruppen*'s Training Department and were provided by Inspectorate office 6. The request had to indicate the expected duration of deployment of the *Lehrkommandos*. If a division requested more than three training detachments, a staff officer was appointed to lead them. He had the task of supervising the training activities and primarily carrying out officer training in the form of simulation games and field briefings.

Training commands for other branches of the armed forces—such as *Panzer-Pioniere* or *Panzer-Artillerie*—were also to be requested from the Training Department.

The *Nachrichtenblatt* went on to warn about the strict standards that had to be applied when requesting training detachments for mechanized infantry units, as the members of the detachments had to be taken from *Panzertruppenschulen* and their training battalions, thus taking away the best instructors from their positions for a period.

Uniforms

Oberleutnant Bodo Spranz, *Batteriechef* of 1./StuG Abt 237, and his crew in front of their StuG 40 Ausf G near Smolensk in 1943. Spranz sports four silver tank-destruction badges (one more and he'll be able to swap them for a gold one) awarded when in StuG-Abt 185; the barrel of his gun has 33 white rings indicating the number of armored vehicles believed destroyed by the crew. His decorations at this date include Wound Badge in Gold (December 8, 1942), Iron Cross (1939), II. Klasse (June 23, 1940), I. Klasse (July 2, 1941), General Assault Badge (February 6, 1941), and German Cross in Gold (May 6, 1943). His crew are also well decorated: the man at left has the EK II and General Assault Badge; to Spranz's left the first man's badges are obscured, but it looks as if he has the General Assault Badge; the next has the EK I and II and General Assault Badge. All wear the *feldgrau*, two-piece *Sturmartillerie* uniform with *Litzen* rather than *Totenköpfe*, and *Panzer* rubber-soled boots; Spranz has a *Schirmmütze* and the others wear M42 *Feldmützen* (sidecaps). Spranz had started the war in Artillerie-Regiment 12 in Poland, went to *Waffenschule* in Jüterbog and, promoted *Leutnant*, fought as a *Zugführer* in IV./Artillerie-Regiment 209 in France. He transitioned to the *Sturmgeschütz* at Jüterbog and became a *Zugführer* in StuG-Abt 185 for *Barbarossa*. He went on to claim over 50 kills, earning himself the Knight's Cross of the Iron Cross with Oak Leaves (October 3, 1943), promotion to *Hauptmann*, and work at the *Sturmgeschützschule* at Magdeburg in 1944; he became a staff officer in 1945. Postwar he became director of the ethnological museum in Freiburg and lived until 2007. (waralbum.ru)

Left and Above left: From the belongings of a soldier with a Putlos tank shooting school identification tag, this photo shows him wearing the M36 *Panzer* wrapover jacket in field gray for *Sturmartillerie* crew, field-gray shirt, and black tie. On the collar is the *Totenkopf* on a dark-green base with red piping (the *Waffenfarbe* of the artillery—"Danziger"-type *Totenköpfe* on a *feldgrau* base with red piping shown at left). In 1943 these were phased out and replaced with the standard *Litzen* collar tabs. On his left breast are the EK I, a General Assault Badge for supporting infantry three times on separate days, and a black wound badge. A cuff-title is partially visible on his left arm. He wears fur-lined buckled leather gloves and, on his head, an M43 *Einheitsfeldmütze*. His button-flap trousers appear to be in Italian M29 camouflage—vast amounts fell into German hands with the capitulation of the Italian military in 1943. On his feet are felt-and-leather winter boots (*Winterstiefel*). (www.themarshalsbaton.com; Akira Takiguchi)

Above right: Luftwaffe ground troops were similarly equipped to the German Army. Here an *Obergefreiter* (corporal) sits on the barrel of a 15 cm sIG 33 Grille Ausf H. He's from the "*Weissen Spiegel*"—the "White Mirrors," the Luftwaffe unit that grew from a regiment to become the Fallschirm-Panzerkorps Hermann Göring. All wear the *Fliegerbluse* (which was blue-gray, fly-fronted, with shallow skirt pockets, and the Luftwaffe eagle on the right breast). Note the Hermann Göring cuff-titles and the *Fahnenjunker* silver shoulder slide on the shoulder board of the man at left. (Akira Takiguchi)

As is so often the case with German uniforms, that of the *Sturmartillerie* seems straightforward. The black woolen tanker's uniform with a short, double-breasted *Panzerjacke*, had proved very popular, so the *Sturmartillerie* was given the same thing in *feldgrau* (field gray) in 1941 having been trialed in 1940. It too had hidden buttons and closed cuffs to reduce snagging inside their vehicles. It had a dark-green collar at first and was matched by a *feldgrau* version of the *Schutzmütze* beret with its rubber skull protector. The *feldgrau* was chosen because the black stood out too much when the crews were on foot during reconnaissance sweeps in the front line. It didn't have the collar piping of the *Panzer* version and didn't have the NCO's collar *Tresse*.

That all seems straightforward. Unfortunately, however, things are not quite so easy. (For the researcher, it's also very difficult to be precise about color in a period where so much of the photography was limited to black-and-white images.) First, the *Sturmartillerie* was also originally allocated black uniforms: all AFV crew wore this from its inception in 1934 and the crews of the Panzerjäger I wore the *Panzerdienstanzug*. Second, a man in a *feldgrau Panzerjacke* might not be in the *Sturmartillerie*, because other units wore these uniforms: *Panzer* propaganda companies and engineer battalions; and *Panzerjäger* units using SP guns. Assault gun and tank destroyer units in armored units also wore *feldgrau*. But sometimes they wore black. The *Sturmartillerie* of the Artillerie-Lehr-Regiment Jüterbog wore the black with an "L" applied to the *Schulterstücke*. Sturmgeschützschule Burg had a small "s" on theirs.

Then there are the various *Waffenfarbe* (arm of service colors) associated with the black and *feldgrau* uniforms' *Schulterklappen*, *Schulterstücke* (shoulder boards), and *Kragenspiegel*—the collar patches worn by the Wehrmacht until 1943 when *Litzen* were officially adopted —and the inclusion (or not) in the *Kragenspiegel* of a *Totenkopf* (death's head—a jawless skull).

The Hummel had six crew: commander, driver, radio operator, and three guncrew. Three are shown here along with a Hungarian medical officer. They are wearing various reversible winter camouflage uniforms. From left: a two-piece padded winter parka with hood and trousers in splinter (*Splitter*) camouflage; next, a shorter reversible two-piece parka (the trousers could be *Splitter*) in *Winter Sumpftarn* (marsh 44 pattern). Next, there's a very grubby *Rauchtarnmuster* (smoke pattern) outfit with an unidentified reverse pattern and pull-tabs at the waist. Finally, the medical officer wears the standard Hungarian field service sidecap with turn-down flaps, false peak, twin button front, and cockade. He wears a shortened officer's leather jacket with cuff-ties, Hungarian shield-stamped buttons, a pistol holster and a leather belt, jodhpurs, and spurred riding boots. The Hummel in the background bears the Hans Hummel water-carrier insignia that is a Hamburg trademark. To this day there's a traditional cry—"*Hummel, Hummel*"—to which the reply is "*Mors, Mors*" (Kiss my butt): not so much a greeting as an identifying battle cry used by Hamburg residents, but the unit is unknown. (Akira Takiguchi via Ian Spring/Pixpast.com)

Above left: A *Sturmartillerie* officer wearing a *feldgrau* jacket with an EK II ribbon on the collar, double *Litzen* on dark-green backing, and artillery red *Waffenfarbe*, and an officer's double-claw belt around his waist. Officers were responsible for purchasing their own uniforms and had a clothing allowance. As a private purchase, minor alterations were tolerated. (RCT)

Above: Artillery enlisted man or NCO's *Litzen* collar tabs. They have dark-green backing, matte silver-gray *Litzen* with bright-red stripes. (www.themarshalsbaton.com)

Above right: This privately tailored, custom-made *Sturmartillerie Feldjacke* with matching pants—note single button and tie closure—is made from a fine green tricot (tight weave structure giving a sleek appearance) and lined in gray-green artificial silk. This is the best uniform of an *Oberleutnant* of Panzer-Regiment 6's *Aufklärungs-Abteilung* (reconnaissance) unit with its gold-yellow *Waffenfarbe* piping on shoulder boards and *Litzen*. There's an EK II ribbon stitched to the collar and there are award loops on the lower-left breast. (www.themarshalsbaton.com)

Photographed by SS-Kriegsberichter August Ahrens in the Soviet Union in 1943, an 8. SS-Kavallerie-Division Florian Geyer StuG 40 Ausf G crewman wears the two-piece field-gray assault gun wrap, cut in the SS pattern, and field-gray trousers. He has an EK II ribbon on his lapel and a black wound badge. Underneath his top he wears what looks like a sheepskin jerkin and around his neck a scarf of sorts. His headwear is the M40 field cap. "Florian Geyer" were involved in internal security and *Bandenbekämpfung* (lit. bandit-fighting, antipartisan operations) duties until September 1943. (NARA)

The *Sturmartillerie*'s *Waffenfarbe* was bright red (*hochrot*) and, at first, the *Sturmartillerie*'s uniform featured *Waffenfarbe* in this color along with the skulls that appeared on the tanker's uniform. Originally, the *Sturmartillerie*'s *Kragenspiegel* were dark-green backed. As early as spring 1942, some officers began to apply *Litzen* collar patches to their *Sturmartillerie* uniforms rather than the rectangular *Kragenspiegel*; from January 1943, this became official, and the skulls had to be removed and *Litzen* collar patches (edged in bright red) be employed instead. Many did so—but not all. And, of course, there were other *Waffenfarben* involved from *rosa* (pink) of the armored troops (also worn by *Panzerjäger*) to gold-yellow for reconnaissance, lemon-yellow for signals, grass green for *Panzergrenadiere*, white for infantry, and black and white for *Pioniere*.

The official assault gun uniform came in a range of gray and green shades as the photographs show. The colors depended on where the uniforms were made, the fabric used, wear and tear, whether they were being used in Germany or in the field, and whether they were clothing NCOs or officers. The trousers were like the black *Panzer* version with the patch pockets, drawstring and buttons at the ankles, and a stirrup under the arch. There was a gray tricot pullover shirt that was worn throughout the war although it was officially replaced in January 1944 by the general service gray-green shirt.

The *Verwundetenabzeichen* (wound badge) had three classes although a recipient could bypass the earlier forms if the wound were severe enough or in the event of death. This is the first-class badge, the gold one, that was awarded for five or more wounds. Silver was for three or four, and iron (a black medal) was for one or two wounds. (www.themarshalsbaton.com)

In the summer of 1941 a lighter version of the uniform in field-green

A mid-war photo of young tank and *Sturmartillerie* men—all of whom wear the standard *feldgrau* shirts and black ties. The *Panzermänner* wear M36 black *Panzer* uniforms with *rosa*—pink, for *Panzer*—piping around the shoulder boards and the *Totenkopf* collar tabs but not the collar. Six wear the M40 *Feldmütze* and—at back right—the M43 *Panzer Einheitsfeldmütze*. The *Panzermann* at front left has an SA Sports Badge and what looks like the HJ Proficiency Badge. The *Sturmartillerie* contingent wear the *feldgrau* M36 *Sturmgeschütz* jackets with *Waffenfarbe* piping—*hochrot* for artillery—on shoulder boards and around the *Totenkopf* collar tabs. However, note the man second right of front row has the standard *Litzen* collar tab which replaced the *Totenkopf*. All wear the *feldgrau* M43 field cap. (RCT)

M43 *Feldjacke* for StuG NCO in *feldgrau* wool. Note machine-woven breast eagle, artillery red piping around the collar tabs with "Danziger"-type *Totenköpfe* on a *feldgrau* base (StuG 2), as are the *Tresse*-trimmed, artillery red-piped shoulder boards with the single pip of a *Feldwebel*. (www.themarshalsbaton.com)

drill was used. It proved popular and was used by many AFV crews. Later versions of this had a map pocket on the outside left.

Cold weather gear was important—particularly for those whose duties took them onto draughty open-air gun platforms. Initially, that was provided by a German Army greatcoat:

later in the war there was specific winter wear with reversible double-breasted gray/white or camouflaged/white jacket, trousers, mittens, and toque. Large enough to wear over a service uniform, the reversible uniform was introduced in 1942–43. Camouflage came in both green splinter and tan water patterns. These were used extensively—as were a variety of officially issued or locally acquired anoraks/*Windblusen*/fur coats/camouflaged smocks, and *Zeltbahn* sections.

The headgear was also like that of the *Panzer* crew: *Schirmmütze*, *Einheitsfeldmütze*, and the gray M1934 and M1938 *Feldmützen*—the caps being easier to use with headphones. Note that boots weren't hobnailed but rubber-soled to reduce sparks.

The uniforms of Waffen-SS and Luftwaffe mirrored the army uniforms with similar (but not identical) short jackets and the standard insignia and rank identification. Those of the Luftwaffe were both gray green and blue gray. Those of the Waffen-SS were gray green and either wool or of a lighter herringbone twill—and also used were uniforms in the various Waffen-SS camouflage patterns.

The "boss" of a *Sturmgeschütz* surveys the landscape in front of Kiev. His optics are a Scherenfernrohr 14Z (scissors telescope) invented by the firm Carl Zeiss. These were adjustable twin periscopic extensions connected by a hinge. They could be upright, as here, or splayed for greater depth perception thus causing objects to appear in modeled relief and out of the background. The user/observer remained out of sight inside the vehicle. Note in front of the commander's hatch the top of the gunner's Sfl. ZF1 periscope. Spending time with your head outside the protection of the armored superstructure was an occupational hazard for StuG and tank commanders—one reason why their losses were so high. This one at least wears an M35 rolled rim helmet with screwed-in side-vents. Most times, because you couldn't wear headphones comfortably in a helmet, commanders wore a *Schirmmütze* or field cap. (NARA)

Above: Captured StuG "men"—all under 20 years old—in a PoW camp in Germany. Their American captors have ordered them to unpack their backpacks for inspection—the contents are laid out on *Zeltbahnen*. They wear the *feldgrau Sturmartillerie Feldbluse* and trousers along with the M43 *Feldmütze*. (Ian Spring/Pixpast.com)

Right: Non-reversible Heer winter parka in a water pattern camo (inside is gray rayon). Six large plastic buttons secure an interior flap and the outside panel. (www.themarshalsbaton.com)

Below: General Walther Model in conversation with the crew of a StuG 40 Ausf G on the Eastern Front, January 1943. The attentive soldiers stand in their assorted, filthy uniforms—note the extended fingers rather than the clenched fist. The general's wearing a "crusher" M36 gabardine cap with silvered cord chinstrap; the interior wire has been bent to create a personal shape. True "crushers" have the wire removed to create a shapeless cap that allowed the wearing of headphones. His heavy-duty knee-length winter topcoat has a large collar and pockets for easy access, and a rear adjustable belt. The soldiers are wearing the *Winteranzug*. Note large white canvas winter gauntlets on the man behind Model. (NAC)

Left: A Panzergrenadier of the Großdeutschland Division standing by the muzzle brake of his assault gun, Eastern Front, 1944. He wears the reversible splinter-pattern winter jacket. (GF Collection)

Below left: Among the German PoWs in this April 1945 photograph taken at Menden in the Ruhr is, center, the monocled Oberstleutnant Heinz Günther Guderian (son of "Schnelle Heinz"), 1a (Operations Officer) of 116. Panzer-Division Windhund, after he had been captured by men of U.S. Seventh Army in 1945. He wears the standard M1942 black uniform jacket (though the collar piping was removed from this issue) with *Litzen* rather than skulls on the collar patches; an officer's belt; an M1938 officer's field cap; has the Knight's Cross which he was awarded on October 5, 1944, at his neck; and the silver *Panzerkampfabzeichen*, a silver DRL sport badge, and a silver wound badge on his left breast. Next to him is Windhund's adjutant, Major Fritz Vogelsang, wearing the *feldgrau Panzerjäger* uniform and on his head the officer's version of the M43 *Einheitsfeldmütze* with a metal-type *Hoheitsabzeichen* pinned above the cockade. At the rear left a faded camo jacket; right a reversible winter jacket and *Telo Mimetico* Italian pattern camo trousers introduced early 1943. (NARA)

Above left and Left: Chief of staff to XIII. SS-Armeekorps SS-Obersturmbannführer Albert Ekkehard and an unknown Waffen-SS officer talk to Lt. Col. Leslie Crozier Wood of 101st Mechanized Cavalry Group and a U.S. Army translator during the surrender of Waffen-SS forces in Schwendt, Austria, May 9, 1945. Ekkehard wears an officer's quality M36 *feldgrau* short uniform jacket and M36 *steingrau* trousers with vertical side pockets tucked into rubber-soled *Panzer* boots that gave better grip inside armored vehicles. The German Cross in Gold is on his right breast. He also wears an M43 field cap with silver-braid piping. Next to him is an *SS-Hauptsturmführer* (captain) wearing an M36 *Sturmgeschütz* wrap with an EK II ribbon on his lapel and brown officer's belt with a two-claw buckle, and M36 trousers as well. His *Waffenfarbe* is possibly golden yellow representing cavalry/reconnaissance. His fiber-peaked *feldgrau* white-piped M32 cap has been "molded" by bending the interior wire to create an "original," personal look. This wasn't particularly original as most wearers did it. At right an artillery officer's cap of *feldgrau* wool with red piping, black Vulkan-fiber visor, and silver-aluminum bullion chin cords, cap eagle, wreath, and cockade. (Ian Spring/Pixpast.com; www.themarshalsbaton.com)

Above right: Sitting on a Panzerjäger I this soldier wears a button-front, one-piece overall over his uniform. There were many different variations—pockets, no pockets, zip or buttons, ankle ties or not, hoods etc. The advantage of the one-piece was less snagging when getting in or out through hatches and it protected the uniform when maintaining or repairing tank parts. Footwear is the M43 *Schnürschuhe* (low boots) with lace-hooks and leather soles. Note the lack of studs/hobnails. On his head the M34 field cap which was popular with armored vehicle crews because it allowed unobstructed use of headphones and optics. Panzerjägerabteilung (Sfl) 643 had three companies, each with nine Panzerjäger I tank destroyers. It was later absorbed into the Großdeutschland Division. (Akira Takiguchi)

Right: A black wool based M34 Panzer overseas cap with artillery red soutache (inverted V trimming) cockade, and stitched eagle. Note aluminum grommet/vent on the side. (www.themarshalsbaton.com)

Many 7.62 cm field guns were captured from the Red Army. Powerful antitank weapons, they made effective SP tank destroyers when married to the PzKpfw 38(t) chassis. These Marder IIIs are from Panzerjägerabteilung 158 of 58. Infanterie-Division. The one on left has four patches on its gunshield. Note the gun lock, muzzle protector, and hull-mounted 7.92 mm MG. The serious-looking crews of the two vehicles wear an impressive display of uniforms. From left:

1. A well-worn M41 *Feldbluse* (jacket). These lacked the green collar and had six buttons rather than the five of earlier, better-quality versions. His toque, a *feldgrau* shapeless sleeve open at both ends, is rolled up over his M42 *Feldmütze*. His baggy, reversible mouse-gray winter uniform overtrousers came with a similar jacket. The combination was introduced during winter 1942/43 from bitter experience the year before. He looks to have canvas gaiters over his boots and reversible winter mittens.

2. This man wears a M40 *Feldbluse*. It too had no green collar, five buttons, and four pleated three-pointed pocket flaps. Around the neck is his toque, on his head an M42 *Feldmütze*, and he wears buckled winter mittens. His baggy overtrousers are tucked into thick felt-and-leather winter boots.

3. Another M40 *Feldbluse*, this one adorned with a medal ribbon from second buttonhole and a flashlight torch; again, baggy winter overtrousers are tucked into *Winterstiefel*; this man's M42 *Feldmütze* sits over his toque.

4 and 5. These two men wear the mouse-gray padded reversible parka winter jacket, part of the winter suit (*Winteranzug*) developed and designed in 1942 by Joseph Neckermann. Three million units were manufactured and chemically treated to increase water resistance. It has a reversible waist tie, not seen, two pockets, six pebble-finish buttons, buttoned cuff, unlined hood big enough to fit over a helmet, bottom hem cord, and reinforced elbows. The man on the left has rolled his cuffs and wears mittens. His winter suit trousers (*Winterhose*) are laced over his boots while his mate's are tucked in. Both have their toques over their heads and necks and wear *Feldmützen*.

6. He has an issued *Pelzmütze* (fur hat) or a Soviet fur *Ushanka*, a jerkin over his jacket, mittens, and baggy *Winteranzug* trousers over his boots.

7. The officer in the foreground wears the M42 light-gray *Winteranzug* and felt-and-leather *Winterstiefel*. His sidearm is on his hip and he has officers' fur-lined gloves.

8. An *Unteroffizier* (sergeant) wears a M36 *Feldbluse* with an EK II ribbon from a buttonhole, a black wound badge (one or two wounds), and a what looks like a General Assault Badge. He's wearing overly large gloves and padded trousers over felt-and-leather *Winterstiefel*. (Akira Takiguchi)

Medals and Awards

Soldiers need awards and decorations. They show themselves and their peer group that they have been recognized and honored. Medals motivate: they were worn at the front so that everyone could see them (except, possibly, the *Bandenkampfabzeichen* which in the wrong circumstances could get you lynched). Michaelis noted in *Deutsche Kriegsauszeichnungen*: "An Estonian volunteer remarks: 'For us Estonians it was understood to defend our home country. We did not want any awards—we wanted freedom! We often had to grin when we saw our German comrades counting how many attacks they still needed to receive the Close Combat Clasp.'"

Most of the medals awarded to StuG, *Artillerie*, and *Panzerjäger* crews were the same as those given to tank crew and to the German Army as a whole. Most images of *Sturmgeschütz* or *Panzerartillerie* personnel have the various Iron Crosses (the ribbon appearing on the left breast on the left collar flap edge), *Deutsches Kreuz in Gold*, *Ehrenblattspange des Heeres*, assault badges, wound badges, tank destruction badges, the *Nahkampfspange*, the *Ostmedaille*, campaign shields, and the *Anerkennungsurkunde des Oberbefehlshabers des Heeres*. The latter—the Certificate of Appreciation of the Commander in Chief of the Army for Outstanding Achievements on the Battlefield—was established on September 6, 1941, and was awarded to personnel in the army and the Waffen-SS. Up till late 1941 it was signed by GFM Walter von Brauchitsch; after he was dismissed, Hitler took over.

Unteroffizier Horst Naumann of 3./StuG-Abt 184 in March 1943 being awarded the *Ritterkreuz des Eisernen Kreuzes* (Knight's Cross of the Iron Cross), the lowest of four grades of Germany's highest award, for destroying six Soviet tanks while commanding his *Sturmgeschütz* in defense of the corridor to the Demyansk salient in January 1943 (and, incidentally, taking his total score to 26). He also has the EK I. Klasse and *Allgemeines Sturmabzeichen* (General Assault Badge) pinned to his double-breasted jacket. Postwar he served with the Bundeswehr. After early 1943 the *Panzer*-style *Totenkopf* collar patches gave way to the standard army *Litzen*. (Fotocollectie Spaarnestad Underwerpe/Nationaalarchief)

The silver *Panzerkampfabzeichen* had been instituted on December 20, 1939, for tank crew who had participated in three armored attacks on separate days. On June 1, 1940, a bronze version was created for *Panzergrenadiere*, elements of *Panzer-Divisionen* who didn't fight in tanks, and from December 31, 1942, tank maintenance teams in the combat area. StuG and *Panzerjäger* crew would have received the bronze version of the award.

The Feldherrnhalle had important connotations for the Nazis. It was at the Feldherrnhalle monument in Munich that the final skirmish of Hitler and the embryonic Nazi Party's Beer Hall Putsch ended. The location was revered after the NSDAP came to power and on June 20, 1943, its name was given to the Panzergrenadier division created from 60. Infanterie-Division that had been destroyed at Stalingrad. Many of its recruits were members of—or had been trained by—the SA. The new division was also decimated, this time as part of Heeresgruppe Mitte during Operation *Bagration* in July 1944. The photo was taken on September 11, 1944, during a training exercise in Elbing, West Prussia, as the unit was recreated again. It would become the Panzergrenadier-Division Feldherrnhalle on November 27, 1944, and once more be destroyed—this time at Budapest in February 1945—and revivified.

This fascinating photograph shows a variety of Feldherrnhalle personnel in their distinctive uniform with the unit's cuff-title (*Ärmelstreifen*—always worn on the left arm) and collar patch incorporating the *Wolfsangel* rune over a carmine-red patch. (The SA version had a central SA logo.) From left: an *Oberfeldwebel* (sergeant major) with his whistle lanyard and Feldherrnhalle cuff-title; the collar patches are magenta in color. He wears an EK II ribbon and probably an Ostfront ribbon from his top buttonhole; on his left breast there's an EK I, an Infantry Assault Badge (*Infanterie Sturmabzeichen*) and what appears to be a well-worn black wound badge (third class for one or two wounds). There's no breast eagle on his tunic nor on the man to his left. The *Feldwebel* in the center of the photograph—note NCO's silver *Tressen* (braid) around the collar and shoulder boards and *Schirmmütze* with shiny leather chinstrap—has an unusually bent breast eagle and a medal bar—note that his second button down is unbuttoned for his notebook.

Next there's an officer from a *Sturmgeschütz* or *Panzerjäger* unit wearing the special two-piece field-gray uniform which was identical to the *Panzertruppe* black uniform. He has an officer's *Schirmmütze* with silver chinstrap. The medal ribbons on his lapel are the EK II and the War Service Cross (*Kriegsverdienstkreuz*), just beneath, a medal bar. Below he has a black wound badge, the General Assault, and a bronze SA Sports Badge. In 1939 Hitler changed the name of this award from SA Sports Badge to *SA-Wehrabzeichen* (SA-Defense Badge) and expected all able-bodied boys from 16 and older to compete for it. It was a more important award then than we'd credit today.

Finally, at right there's a highly decorated *SA-Hauptsturmführer/Rittermeister* (captain) wearing the Feldherrnhalle cuff-title, medal ribbons on his lapel, and various medals. These appear to be the General Assault Badge, EK I, SA Sports Badge in silver, an Infantry Assault Badge in silver, a Silver Wound Badge (for being wounded three to four times), and a Silver DRL Sports Badge (*Deutscher Reichsbund für Leibesübungen*). He wears an M43 *Einheitsfeldmütze* field cap with silver (officer's) piping around the crown. The belts seen are the two-clawed buckle type for senior NCOs and officers. (Akira Takiguchi)

Above left: Hauptmann Peter Frantz, holder of the *Ritterkreuz mit Eichenlaub* (Knight's Cross with Oak Leaves), also wears the *Deutsches Kreuz in Gold* (German Cross in Gold) on his right breast, which was awarded for repeated acts of bravery or exceptional leadership. Frantz was commander of the *Sturmgeschütz* detachment of the Panzergrenadier-Division Großdeutschland (note the 1940 Großdeutschland cuff-title at left) and was awarded the *Eichenlaub* to his *Ritterkreuz* for his actions during the third battle of Kharkov in March 1943. In August 1944, after going to the Kriegsakademie, he became *Quartiermeister* on the staff of XXXXI. Panzerkorps before surrendering to the U.S. Army in 1945. (Fotocollectie Spaarnestad Underwerpe/Nationaalarchief)

Above right: Oberwachtmeister Richard Schramm of 1./StuG-Abt 202 wears the Knight's Cross he received for destroying 12 Soviet tanks in late 1942 around Sychyovka, northeast of Smolensk. His StuG has been appropriately named *Seeteufel*, the sea-devil or angler-fish. Note his rank: *Sturmgeschütz* crew carried artillery ranks. *Oberwachtmeister* is the equivalent of *Oberfeldwebel* (master sergeant). Schramm has the double bar on his shoulder straps indicating a potential officer (*Offizieranwarter*). He wears the *feldgrau* (field-gray) double-breasted uniform. Schramm went MIA in the second battle of Kurland in late 1944 and was presumed dead. (Fotocollectie Spaarnestad Underwerpe/Nationaalarchief)

The General Assault Badge (pictured left) was awarded to men from units who supported infantry in combat but who weren't eligible for the Infantry Assault Badge—particularly men of the *Artillerie*. It was not uncommon to see StuG and *Panzerjäger* crew wearing this badge and the famous *Panzerknacker*—tank destruction—strip arm badge(s). While these were not awarded to AFV gunners, many gunners won the awards when fighting outside their vehicles.

The Vehicles

Sturmgeschütze

The StuG III came in two main versions: early, armed with an L/24 7.5 cm main gun; late, armed with a *Langrohr* L/43 or L/48. The early versions, Ausf A–E, were produced up to 1942: 850 in total; the Ausf F, F/8, and G from March 1942 onward in large numbers: 360 Fs, 250 F/8s, and over 8,000 Gs. For local defense the crew carried small arms and there was the usual *Nebelkerzenabwurfvorrichtung* rear-mounted smoke candle dispenser that was activated from inside. This was replaced in 1942 by the *Nebelwurfgerät* (two banks of three dischargers on each side of the vehicle) and, finally, by the *Nahverteidigungswaffe* launcher which could launch smoke rounds or be used for close-in defense. StuGs could also fire smoke rounds from their main gun.

- **Ausf A:** Used in the battle of France; based on the PzKpfw III Ausf G, they retained the hull-side escape hatches.
- **Ausf B:** Various drivetrain changes and a six-speed gearbox.
- **Ausf C and D:** Gunner's forward view port above driver's visor in the A and B was a shot trap and was eliminated; instead, gunner's periscopic Sfl ZF1 gunsight was moved to superstructure top requiring changes to the gunner's roof hatch.

This Sturmgeschütz Ausf A can be seen at the Australian Armour and Artillery Museum. It has been heavily restored by Dmitry Bushmakow Restoration, Czechia. It's the only one of the 36 Ausf As known to exist. It was lost in the Shosha River while part of StuG-Btr 660. The museum cites "7,000 kilometers in a Sturmgeschuetz," the wartime diary of *Ritterkreuzträger* Heinrich Engel, as mentioning that he lost an Ausf A there. The museum vehicle wears the tactical markings and the insignia (the *Totenkopf*) of 2./StuG-Abt 192 for June 1941, the beginning of Operation *Barbarossa*. (Australian Armour and Artillery Museum, Cairns)

StuG III Ausf B. Note the shuttered gunner's direct viewing port which was eliminated on the Ausf C. The photograph gives a good closeup of the covered headlights, the driver's periscope holes, and vision port below. The Notek convoy light is at right (see also p. 83). (GF Collection)

- **Ausf D:** Onboard intercom installed.
- **Ausf E:** Superstructure sides extended to provide boxes for radio equipment. This also increased ammo carried to 50. Commanders officially provided with SF14Z scissors periscopes. Major changes to communications (see p. 82).
- **Ausf F:** The first Ausf to carry the longer 7.5 cm StuK 40 L/43 main gun. Exhaust fan added to the rooftop to evacuate firing fumes. From June 1942, additional 30 mm armor plates were welded to the frontal armor, increasing it to 80 mm thick. Also from June, the StuK 40 L/48 came in and became standard.
- **Ausf F/8:** From May 1943 5 mm thick *Schürzen* were added to protect the sides of the

StuG III Ausf C or D. Note alteration to gunner's sight, now a single periscope. Behind are the commander's donkey ears. (NARA)

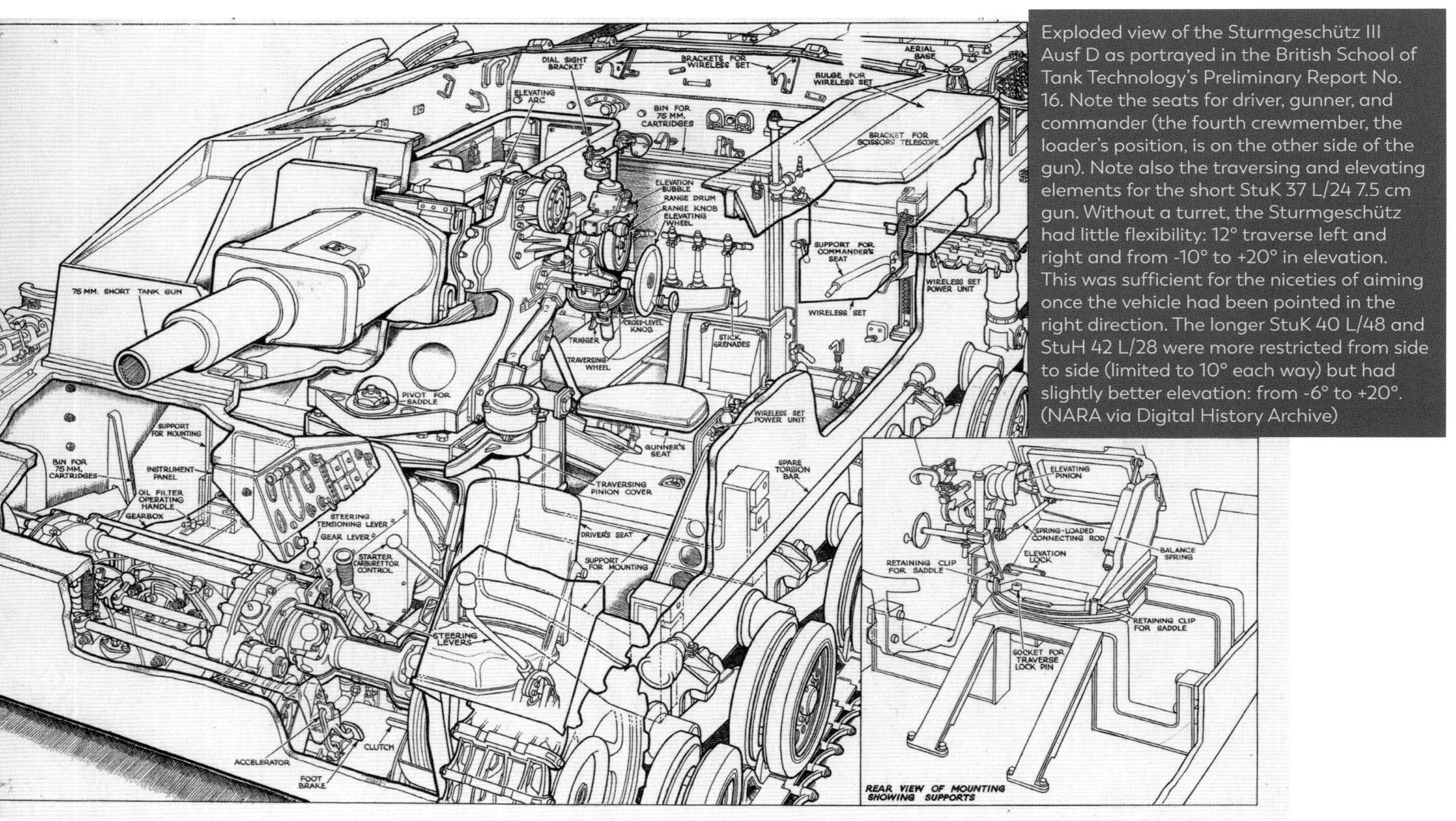

Exploded view of the Sturmgeschütz III Ausf D as portrayed in the British School of Tank Technology's Preliminary Report No. 16. Note the seats for driver, gunner, and commander (the fourth crewmember, the loader's position, is on the other side of the gun). Note also the traversing and elevating elements for the short StuK 37 L/24 7.5 cm gun. Without a turret, the Sturmgeschütz had little flexibility: 12° traverse left and right and from -10° to +20° in elevation. This was sufficient for the niceties of aiming once the vehicle had been pointed in the right direction. The longer StuK 40 L/48 and StuH 42 L/28 were more restricted from side to side (limited to 10° each way) but had slightly better elevation: from -6° to +20°. (NARA via Digital History Archive)

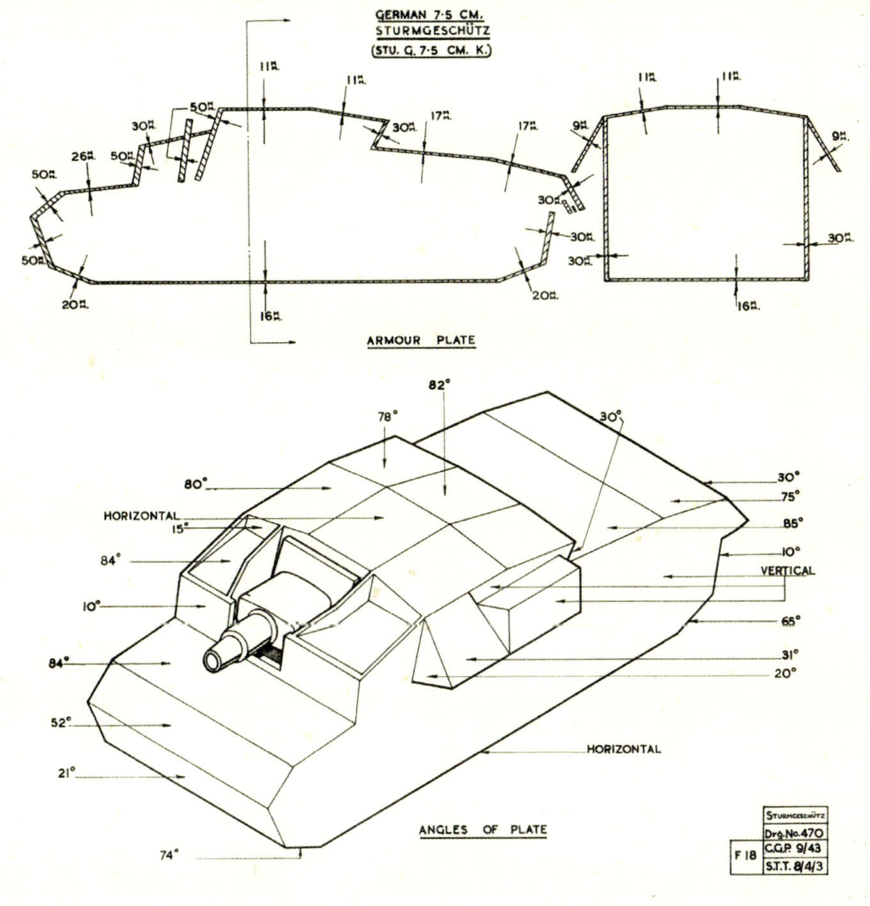

Armor thicknesses of the Ausf D and angles of the plating—the same hull design as the Ausf A was continued through to the Ausf F. From the Ausf F/8 an improved hull like that of the PzKpfw III Ausf J/L saw armor thicknesses improved, particularly the front that had 30 mm appliqué armor riveted to the hull and superstructure. (NARA via Digital History Archive)

vehicle from Soviet antitank rifles. Rear decking hatches were altered and the deck extended farther back.

- **Ausf G:** MIAG joined Alkett in production from February 1943. Hull remained the same, but superstructure modified and made wider and taller. Commander's cupola added and, from October 1943, shot deflectors were added. The rooftop exhaust fan moved to rear. MG shield provided for loader. From March 1943, the driver's periscope was abandoned. From October 1943, the *Topfblende* pot mantlet (today usually referred to as the *Saukopf*—pig's head) gun mantlet was introduced, at first without a coaxial mount,

The Ausf F was the first of *Langrohr* StuG 40s, employing initially the StuK 40 L/43 and then the longer L/48. Among the typical clutter of equipment stowed on backs and sides, an LSSAH (at that time SS-Panzergrenadier-Division Leibstandarte SS Adolf Hitler) crewmember uses a pintle-mounted MG 34 during the third battle of Kharkov. (NARA)

The StuG III Ausf E program was cut back to allow the Ausf F with the long 7.5 cm main armament. The major improvements on the Ausf E were to the left and right panniers, and the inclusion of an MG 34 to the crew's armament. It didn't have a mounting point and the crewmember who fired it was exposed, but it did allow an element of all-round defense. This photo shows an Ausf E leading a PzKpfw II and a PzKpfw III. (GF Collection)

Sturmgeschütz 40 Ausf F as restored by Dmitry Bushmakow. This is believed to be the only existing StuG Ausf F and may have been part of StuG-Abt 244 in Stalingrad. Note the Ausf F's main distinguishing feature, the air filter between the commander and loader's hatches. Note, too, the stowage of equipment: (from front to back) sledgehammer, S-shaped towing hook, wire cutters, another hook, and the jack. (Australian Armour and Artillery Museum, Cairns)

Finnish Sturmgeschütz IIIG (Ps 531-18) after battle reenactment display on Adolf Ehrnrooth Square during the Finnish military Flag Day 2014 in Lappeenranta Rakuunamäki. Note camo scheme, gunner's and commander's scopes, MG shield, and Notek light positioned at front of hull. (MKFI/WikiCommons/CC0 1.0)

Rear view of a StuG III Ausf D. Note the spare track and road wheels and the NKAV (*Nebelkerzenabwurfvorrichtung*) smoke dispenser box (1). These were released behind the vehicle from inside. (NARA)

Panzer-Regiment 2 of 16. Panzergrenadier-Division StuG 40 Ausf Gs near the Piazza del Popolo in Rome, Italy, in November 1943. Note the *Nebelwurfgerät* (smoke dispensers—StuGs delivered between February and May 1943 had a set either side of the superstructure), the track links giving extra side protection for the gunner, the commander's cupola without a shot deflector, and the outline tactical numbering. (GF Collection)

rectified early 1944. In September (MIAG) and November (Alkett) 1943 *Zimmerit* was applied. This continued until September 1944. From November 1943 problems with the supply of rubber led to all-metal return rollers being used. In spring 1944 the *Nahverteidigungswaffe* (close-in defense) and rooftop-mounted remote-controlled MG were introduced.

- **Sturmhaubitze 42:** With more and more StuGs being used for *Panzerjäger* duties, the need for an infantry support vehicle reemerged. The first vehicle was designed in 1942—the StuH 42 (SdKfz 142/2). It mounted a variant of the 10.5 cm leFH 18 howitzer that could be modified to be electrically fired and was sometimes fitted with a muzzle brake. The original was based on the Ausf F; production (Alkett built 1,299 between 1943 and 1945) was based on the Ausf G.
- **Sturmgeschütz IV:** After Alkett's works were bombed, Krupp was able to take up the slack by combining the PzKpfw IV chassis with a StuG III Ausf G superstructure modified slightly to provide a suitable extension for the driver. Over 1,000 were produced at the Grusonwerk between end 1943 and early 1945, and the StuG IV equipped many StuG *Abteilungen*.

Arrival of German military reinforcements in Thessaloniki. A column of StuG IVs armed with StuK 40 L/48s passes along the port waterfront among the gathered residents. Note an obvious difference between the StuG IV and StuG 40 Ausf G front: the driver's armored cab. (NAC)

Opposite, above: Top view of the Australian Armour and Artillery Museum's StuG IV. Acquired as a battlefield relic from the Eastern Front, it was rebuilt to its current condition by the museum workshop. While this sort of reconstruction is not always to the aficionados' satisfaction, there's no doubt that most people find the restored exhibit a wonderful recreation of the vehicle allowing the visitor to see details other relics lack. Note here in particular the driver's armored cab and hatch, the stowage of jack and tools, the side structures in place for the addition of *Schürzen*, the hole for the gunner's sight in front of the commander's cupola, and the three-color camouflage scheme that sees a base coat of *dunkelgelb* overlaid with *rotbraun*, and *olivgrün*. (Australian Armour and Artillery Museum, Cairns)

Below: Top view of the StuH 42 in the Australian Armour and Artillery Museum. The lines of the original StuG III chassis are clear, as is the bolted-on appliqué armor. The stumpy main armament of the Sturmhaubitze 42, the 10.5 cm StuH L/28, a modified leFH 18, is also well in evidence. Using two-part ammunition, the StuH had a slower rate of fire than the StuK 40 on which it was based and carried less ammunition (26 HE rounds plus 10 HL/B or C hollow-charge antitank projectiles). This vehicle still has *Zimmerit* in place and, it would appear, a full complement of heavily camouflaged *Schürzen*. Note the appliqué armor added to the driver's position has resulted in the disappearance of his driving periscope. (Australian Armour and Artillery Museum, Cairns)

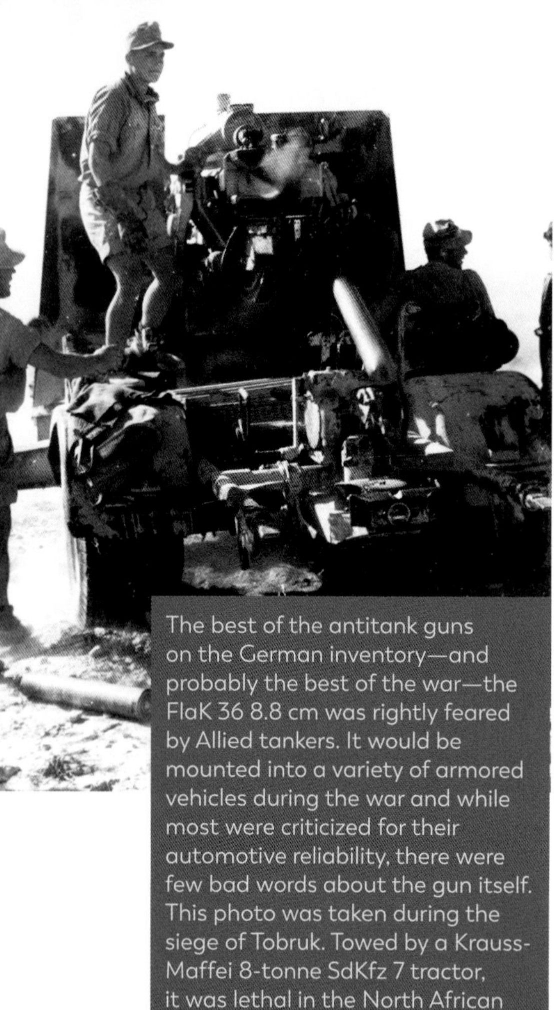

The best of the antitank guns on the German inventory—and probably the best of the war—the FlaK 36 8.8 cm was rightly feared by Allied tankers. It would be mounted into a variety of armored vehicles during the war and while most were criticized for their automotive reliability, there were few bad words about the gun itself. This photo was taken during the siege of Tobruk. Towed by a Krauss-Maffei 8-tonne SdKfz 7 tractor, it was lethal in the North African campaign, outranging Allied equipment. (NARA)

Panzerjäger

In 1939 all German Army divisions had a motorized antitank battalion using towed or hand-delivered weapons: the 3.7 cm PaK 36, 5 cm PaK 38, *Panzerbüchse* antitank rifles, and hand-held explosive charges.

Blitzkrieg, however, showed that the attrition of antitank companies was high and that they needed more mobility and protection (save for the long-range 8.8 cm guns that could stay reasonably clear of the enemy). The answer was the SPG—a tracked chassis mounting an antitank weapon. The first was the Panzerjäger I which saw the Czech 4.7 cm L/43 gun married to a PzKpfw I Ausf B chassis by Alkett (five-sided gunshield) or Klöckner-Humboldt-Deutz (seven-sided). It had a driver and two gunners. Some of the 202 conversions saw action in France, others were sent to Africa (27 equipped Panzerjäger-Abteilung 605), and others took part in *Barbarossa*. They carried 10 HE and 74 antitank rounds but crews complained that there were no periscopes and had to look over the gunshield to acquire targets.

The fall of France provided chassis for antitank guns to be mounted behind gunshields rather than in turrets. The first was along the same lines as the Panzerjäger I but replacing the PzKpfw I chassis: the conversion by Alkett of 174 Renault R35 tanks into the 4.7 cm PaK (t) auf PzKpfw 35R (f) ohne Turm. This took place May–October 1941 and they continued in service in the West into 1944. Considerably cheaper and faster to produce than new tanks, the following *Panzerjäger* came in a variety of shapes and sizes, many of them, confusingly, today named Marder (translates as marten, as in pine marten).

The French Hotchkiss, Renault, or Lorraine 37L chassis captured in France were adapted to mount various weapons, the Lorraine carrier mounting a 7.5 cm PaK 40/1 as the Marder I (24 converted in 1942). The original crew compartment was removed, making room for the larger gun. This meant that a superstructure had to be created to protect the crew—and because armor is heavy, there ended up being not much of either armor or protection from enemy weapons and, as it was open, the elements. Canvas could be rigged to keep some semblance of a dry space but ultimately the gun crew of this sort of vehicle was subjected to the worst of the weather.

The PzKpfw II Ausf D1 and D2 chassis provided the Marder II and was armed with the 7.5 cm PaK 40/2 L/46—about 570 vehicles produced and 75 converted (SdKfz 131, 1942–44). Some 200 were also converted with captured Soviet F-22 7.62 cm L/51.5 guns (SdKfz

Following on from the Panzerjäger I, the next choice of chassis was that of the French Renault R35 two-man tank. The crew was increased to three and a superstructure was built providing armor plate all around (but not on top)—an improvement on the Panzerjäger I's crew protection. There was a command version as well. The vehicles were surprisingly long lived: 110 were still in service in early 1944. This one was knocked out at Le Molay-Littry, probably by men of U.S. 2nd Infantry Division who liberated the twin villages on June 10, 1944. (NARA)

132, 1942–43); in German use, the gun was classified as the PaK 36(r); it was rechambered to take a 7.5 cm round to ensure sufficient ammunition availability, although early vehicles used the original Soviet gun. Rechambering meant increasing the size to accommodate the larger German round which was 33 cm longer and 10 mm wider.

The excellent Czech PzKpfw 38(t) chassis was turned into a *Panzerjäger* by mounting—once large enough numbers had been captured—a Soviet Model 36 7.62 cm as the Marder 38 or III (SdKfz 139). In this form nearly 350 were built, 66 of which were sent to North Africa where it proved very effective. They had to be prepared for desert conditions (mainly filters to reduce the impact of sand on the engine). Some 400 were built using the German 7.5 cm PaK 40/3 L/46 (SdKfz 138). The Marder III's guns could knock out the Soviet T-34 and the early KV-1, although the KV-1A and KV-1B had extra armor and were more difficult.

By the end of 1942/beginning of 1943, many armored and even a few infantry divisions had antitank companies equipped with Marders, but they had drawbacks. The Marder III was

Knocked out during the Lake Balaton battles in Hungary, the commander's hatch of this Jagdpanzer 38(t) is open, showing his placement at the right rear of the vehicle. He sat behind the gun; the rest of the crew was on the other side. The Hungarian 20th Assault Gun Battalion had 15 Hetzer SP guns as well as Zrinyi II and fought at Enying east of the lake. (GF Collection)

Above left: The Marder II made use of the PzKpfw II chassis, the SdKfz 131 mounting a 7.5 cm PaK 40/2 L/48. Note the M38 Fallschirmjäger helmets: several Luftwaffe ground units were equipped with the Marder including Panzer-Artillerie-Regiment Hermann Göring and the various *Panzerjäger-Abteilungen* of the Fallschirmjäger divisions. Note too the MG 34. (GF Collection)

Below left: The SdKfz 132 Marder II matched the 7.62 cm PaK 36(r) with the PzKpfw II Ausf D1 und D2 chassis. This one, seen in September 1943, is from Panzerjäger-Ersatz-und-Ausbildungs-Abteilung 10 that was based in Straubing, Bavaria, Wehrkreis XIII. It provided replacements for several PzJg-Abteilungen. (Akira Takiguchi)

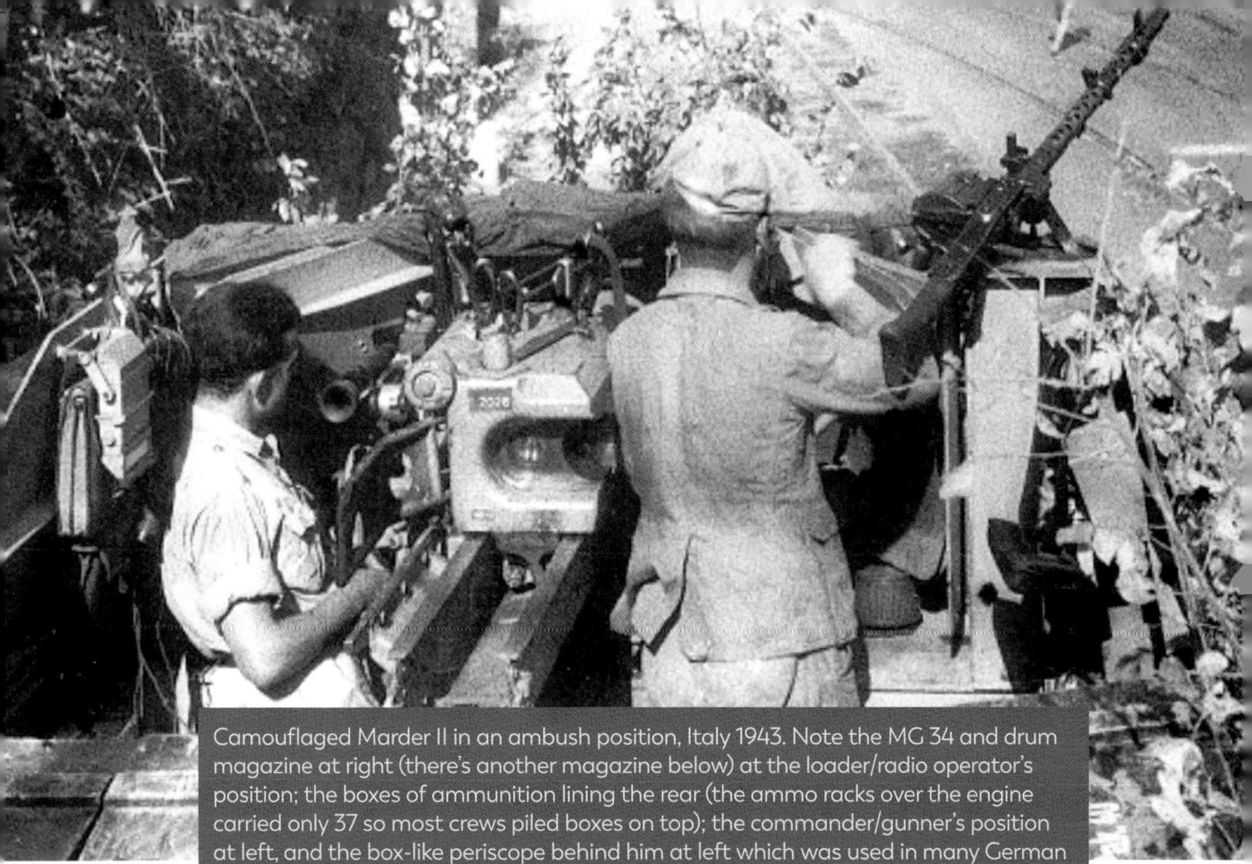

Camouflaged Marder II in an ambush position, Italy 1943. Note the MG 34 and drum magazine at right (there's another magazine below) at the loader/radio operator's position; the boxes of ammunition lining the rear (the ammo racks over the engine carried only 37 so most crews piled boxes on top); the commander/gunner's position at left, and the box-like periscope behind him at left which was used in many German open-topped vehicles to allow a view over the armor plate without exposure to the enemy. (Bundesarchiv, Bild 101I-304-0608-24A/Funke/CC-BY-SA 3.0)

The fighting compartment was a chilly place in winter. Here in the winter of 1942/43 a Marder II waits in a large German column in the Kharkov area. Note the additional boxes of ammunition at the back. The loader is sitting on the gun's recoil shield. (Fotocollectie Spaarnestad Underwerpe/Nationaalarchief)

Marder I is the portmanteau term for the SP *Panzerjäger* created on captured French chassis—mainly Lorraine tractors, and FCM 36 and Hotchkiss H35 tanks—by Alfred Becker's Baukommando in July–August 1942. This 21. Panzer-Division example pairs a 7.5 cm PaK 40 with an H35 chassis. Note the Scherenfernrohr 14Z. (Battlefield Historian)

The cramped fighting platform of the 7.5 cm PaK 40/1 auf Geschützwagen Lorraine Schlepper (f) is apparent on this photograph of a 21. Panzer-Division Marder I. It may have provided little protection to the crew, but its 32° of traverse was better than many Panzerjäger. 21. Panzer's StuG-Abt 200—commanded by the man who had created the conversions, Major Alfred Becker—had 24 Marder Is and proved a thorn in the side of the Allies, particularly during Operation *Goodwood*. (GF Collection)

Men of LSSAH's Panzer-Regiment 1 aboard a Panzerjäger Marder III Ausf H during the third battle of Kharkov, February 1943. Note snow camouflage overalls and other clothing to beat the extreme temperatures. The fighting platforms were open to the freezing air and were cold and wet places to fight. This version was armed with a PaK 40 and retained the Czech hull MG. With a centrally placed fighting compartment it afforded better protection than the Ausf G from a fixed casemate. (Bundesarchiv, Bild 101III-Roth-173-01/ Roth, Franz/CC-BY-SA 3.0)

Marder III Ausf M on the Italian Front. Probably the best of the three versions, the Ausf M saw the engine moved to the midsection with the fighting compartment sinking down to where the engine had been. This meant better crew protection, although the armor was still only 10–15 mm thick. The driver stayed in a compartment in front while the radio operator moved back into the fighting compartment. Most Marder IIIs had an FuSpr. D radio with the command vehicle having an FuG 8 as well. (NAC)

The Jagdpanzer 38(t) at the Australian Armour and Artillery Museum carries the *Fahrgestellnummer* 323437, was built by Skoda in January 1945 and knocked out near Prague in May 1945. It was rebuilt postwar as a G13 for the Swiss Army. However, the vehicle underwent an 18-month restoration project by Axis Track Services in the UK to restore it to its 1945 condition before delivery to the museum in March 2015. Note the three-color camouflage, the remote-controlled MG, gunner's sight, and the black rectangular strips that were designed to fool opponents where the driver's episcopes were. (Australian Armour and Artillery Museum, Cairns)

front-heavy, underpowered and—as with all the early conversions—had a high silhouette. The first two problems could be cured by moving the gun to the back and the engine to the middle. Nearly 1,000 of this version were built in 1943–44 although little could be done to reduce the high silhouette. The PzKpfw 38(t) chassis would also go on to mount a 7.5 cm PaK in an armored superstructure as the Jagdpanzer 38 (we call it the Hetzer today)—2,500+ built in April 1944–May 1945.

In reality, German industry couldn't keep up with the demand for antitank guns and increasingly as the war progressed the infantry had to rely on the *Panzerschreck*, officially the Raketenpanzerbüchse 54, an 8.8 cm rocket launcher similar to the U.S. Army's bazooka that would equip the 1944 Volksgrenadier and 1945 Grenadier *Regimenter* in place of towed antitank guns.

The workhorse of the *Panzerwaffe*, the PzKpfw IV chassis—along with drive components from the PzKpfw III—produced the Geschützwagen III/IV (Sf) chassis designed by Alkett. It mounted an 8.8 cm PaK 43/1 L/71 as the Hornisse, later renamed the Nashorn. The Hummel used the same chassis, and the drawbacks for both were automotive. Nevertheless, the gun allowed long-distance kills out of range of most Allied weapons. 475 were built in 1943–44.

In 1944, the PzKpfw IV chassis was also used for other *Panzerjäger* conversions: over 1,000 of the SdKfz 187 Sturmgeschütz IV, 770 of the SdKfz 167 Jagdpanzer IV (with a 7.5 cm PaK 39 L/48 gun), and over 1,200 with the longer L/70 gun—the PzKpfw IV/70, better known as "Guderian's duck." The IV/70 (SdKfz 162/1) was built in two versions, by Vomag (930 August 1944–March 1945) and Alkett (278). The Jagdpanzer IVs had a low silhouette—if anything, too low: they had problems sighting over hedgerows and walls—and never

The PzKpfw IV/70(V) at the Australian Armour and Artillery Museum was rebuilt by the museum workshop using relics recovered from battlefields of the Eastern Front and sports the late-war ambush camouflage. Note the arc of the gunner's periscope, the commander's Scherenfernrohr 14Z periscope, the *Nahverteidigungswaffe* opening next to the commander's hatch, and the loader's open hatch. (Australian Armour and Artillery Museum, Cairns)

This is the rare Alkett version of the PzKpfw IV/70(A)—which accounts for the (A) rather than (V) for Vomag in the designation. The most obvious distinguishing mark is that the superstructure was higher than the Vomag version. The Alkett version stood at 7 ft 3 in (2.2 m) high; the Vomag at 6 ft 1 in (1.85 m). This 7./Panzer-Regiment 2 Jagdpanzer was destroyed on February 8, 1945, in Mittelwihr, France in the Colmar Pocket. (NARA)

Another excellent overview from the Australian Armour and Artillery Museum, this one a reconstructed Jagdpanther. Rebuilt by the museum workshop from battlefield relics recovered from the Eastern Front, this Jagdpanther is made up, as they say, "of a mixture of fabricated parts, 'new' old stock (armor plate recovered from a recently unearthed tank factory outside of Berlin) and a wreck out of Königsberg (Museum)." The cluttered roof space has a range of interesting features that the attached overlay explains:

1 Gunner's sight
2 *Nahverteidigungswaffe*
3 Viewing block
4 Spikes upon which an EM 0.9 m R "scissors" rangefinder (stowed internally) can be erected
5 Hatch
6 Fume extractor's armor guard
7 Loader's rotating vision block
8 Vent hole with armor guard (this was moved to front of vehicle in one version)
9 Commander's hatch
10 Vision block
11 Commander's 360° viewing block which also has a periscope hatch for the Scherenfernrohr 14Z.

Note the driver's single viewing slit. In earlier models the driver had two with a rain deflector above.

(Australian Armour and Artillery Museum, Cairns)

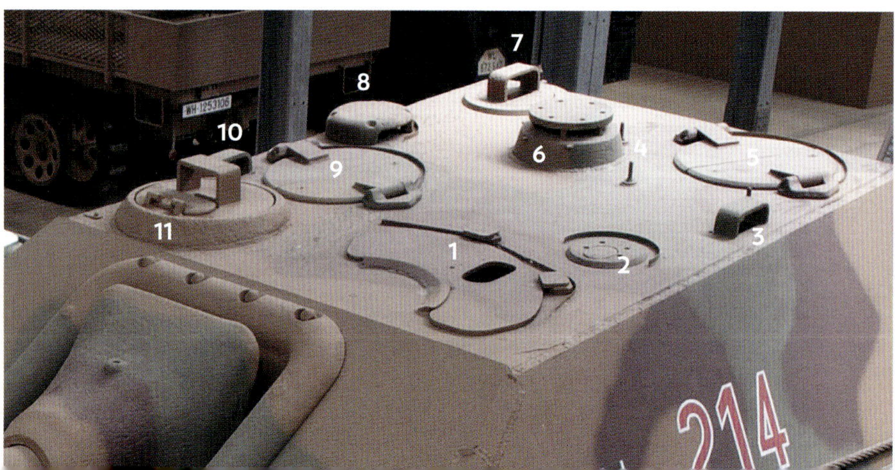

overcame the automotive problems engendered by having so much weight at the front of the vehicle.

Spring 1943 saw the arrival of the Ferdinand, which was renamed the Elefant in 1944. It mounted the 8.8 cm PaK 43/2 L/71, the same gun as in the later Hornisse, renamed the Nashorn, and Tiger II. Finally, the ultimate *Panzerjäger* were the Jagdpanther and the immense Jagdtiger with its 12.8 cm PaK 44 L/55.

The Ferdinand/Elefant (91), Hornisse/Nashorn (494), Jagdpanther (413), and Jagdtiger (about 80)—(production figures in brackets)—equipped the *sPzJg-Abteilungen*. They proved excellent tank killers as they were supposed to but there were too few of them to affect the outcome of the war and they were rushed into combat before all their problems were completely solved. They attract—for understandable reasons, perhaps—more attention today than the workaday StuGs or *Jagdpanzers* that formed the backbone of the *Panzerjäger* force.

Commander of a sPzJg-Abt 654 Jagdpanther in summer 1944 surveying the Normandy countryside from his hatch. In front of him his 360° traversable periscope with *Scherenfernrohr* peeping out in front. He's wearing a splinter camouflage jacket and a *feldgrau* M36 field cap, headphones and throat microphone. (Bundesarchiv, Bild 101I-721-0397-12/Wagner/CC-BY-SA 3.0)

Inside a Jagdpanther, looking from the commander's position across the gun with the loader at left (there were two seats for the loader: one behind the commander and one behind the gunner. Note the lock for the rear hatch in the top center of the photo and the rack of 8.8 cm ammunition. The *Gefreiter* at left—probably the loader—is wearing a *Sturmartillerie* jacket with *Totenkopf Litzen*. The *Waffenfarbe* will be *rosa*—pink—of the *Panzerjäger*. The man at right is probably the gunner having moved back from his seat which was farther forward. He wears standard army shirt and field cap. (GF Collection)

Nashorn *131 Red* in the Patriot Museum, Kubinka—one of only three Nashorns to survive, it's been repainted in an accurate if unusual color scheme. Difficult to hide at 27 ft 8 in (8.44 m) long over the gun barrel by 8 ft 8 in (2.65 m) tall—a Sherman's around 19 ft 5 in (5.92 m) x 9 ft (2.74 m)—it had three men on the gundeck, gunner, loader, and commander with driver and radio operator under armor. Radios were as the Marder: an FuSpr. D with the command vehicle having an FuG 8 as well. (Michel Blinoff)

The fighting compartment of the Nashorn was roomier than many of the *Panzerjäger* platforms, but ammunition load was still small: usually around 40 with 16 in two side lockers and the rest on the floor. Note the commander's Scherenfernrohr 14Z on side mounting and the gunner's sight. (GF Collection)

The Panzerjäger Tiger (P) mit 8.8 cm PaK 43/2 is better known as the Ferdinand, under which name the 90 vehicles were produced, or the Elefant—the name was changed in May 1944. With 10 cm armor plates bolted to the front, its weight—65 tonnes—meant it lacked mobility, found most bridges wanting, and was almost impossible to recover if something went wrong unless there were at least four SdKfz 9 FAMOs handy (and there usually weren't). Its six-man crew (note driver's head in goggles sticking out of hatch at right) liked the overhead protection so many *Panzerjäger* lacked. (GF Collection)

The "Sturer Emil" (Stubborn Emil) was an experimental heavy *Panzerjäger* which paired the Rheinmetall 12.8 cm K 40 L/61 gun with the Henschel VK 30.01 chassis. This one is *Moritz* that ended up in the Kubinka Tank Museum. The fighting compartment was open to the elements but sizable—although this didn't mean that the crew of four (the fifth, the driver, had his own compartment at the front) had a great deal of space because the immense gun—a development of the FlaK 40—took up most of it. It fired two-piece ammunition, and after training at Jüterbog the two vehicles joined PzJr-Abt 521. (U.S. Army)

Abandoned Jagdtiger X7 of sPzJg-Abt 512 in Netphen, Germany, in April 1945. This vehicle—commanded by Lt. Sepp Tarlach—was probably hit by friendly fire, two Panzerfaust rounds, and was the fifth of 10 Jagdtigers lost in four days. (NARA)

Top view of the Jagdtiger's superstructure. 1. Commander's 360° periscope; 2. Escape and observation hatch; 3. Ventilator; 4. Fixed periscopes; 5. Fixed periscope and antenna; 6. 360° periscope; 7. *Nahverteidigungswaffe*; 8. Sliding plate for gunsight. (NARA)

5

Panzerartillerie

The first SP gun for the *Panzer-Divisionen* was the 15 cm sIG 33 (Sf) auf Panzerkampfwagen I Ausf B, better known as the Sturmpanzer I or Bison. It took the standard heavy infantry gun and placed it, rather precariously, on the chassis of the PzKpfw I Ausf B. The gun performed well, the chassis less so. Only 38 conversions were made and so another attempt to carry the same gun was made with the sIG 33 auf Fahrgestell Panzerkampfwagen II (Sf). (This is sometimes referred to as Sturmpanzer II Bison.) The 12 trial vehicles were produced late by Alkett, in January and February 1942, and went to North Africa.

As the Sturmpanzer II also had proved unsuccessful, another attempt was made in 1942. At the end of October, the first of 24 of the Sturm-Infanteriegeschütz 33B (sIG 33B)—the sIG 33/1 mounted on a StuG III chassis—was delivered. (Using *Sturmpanzer* logic, this is occasionally referred to as Sturmpanzer III.) Again, the vehicle was found wanting.

The continuing need for infantry support led to a further development in 1943—with an even bigger gun to allow better use in urban conditions. Known by the Allies as the *Brummbär* and its German users as the "Stupa 43," the Sturmpanzer IV mounted a hefty 15 cm Sturmhaubitze 43 L/12 gun on a PzKpfw IV chassis. Just over 300 were built and equipped four *Sturmpanzer-Abteilungen*. Designed as an infantry support gun, the Sturmpanzer IV was placed under the control of the *Panzertruppen*.

Another obvious candidate for use as an SP gun chassis, the Czech PzKpfw 38(t) had already proved its worth in the opening months of *Barbarossa* when, along with its sister 35(t), it had been used in large numbers. Obsolescent by 1942 as a front-line tank, it made a suitable chassis for use with captured Soviet 7.62 cm (the PaK 36(r) in German service) guns for the *Panzerjäger* and the sIG 33 as an artillery SP gun—the Grille (= cricket); this became known as the Ausf H (engine to the rear = *hinten* in German; 200 converted). The rebuilt

Bison fighting in Hangest-sur-Somme in June 1940 clearly showing the lack of crew protection, the cumbersome nature of the gun carriage, and lack of space for ammunition: only three rounds were carried. (Library of Congress)

This photograph shows how the superstructure fitted around the 15 cm sIG 33 which was placed on the back of PzKpfw I Ausf B chassis without removing the gun from its carriage. (Akira Takiguchi)

Only 24 sIG 33Bs were produced as heavy infantry support weapons. Repainted, one is now in the Kubinka Tank Museum. Note the gunsight port cover on top, the appliqué armor adding 30 mm to the existing 50 mm, and the inspection hatches that show the chassis was originally a later-series StuG. (Alan Wilson/ WikiCommons/CC BY-SA 4.0)

Saumur's "Stupa 43" mounted a hefty 15 cm Sturmhaubitze 43 L/12 gun on a PzKpfw IV chassis. Note the *Zimmerit*, Notek light, ball-mount for machine gun, and—just visible above the top of the superstructure—the commander's cupola, the latter two indicative of a later-model vehicle. The crew of five were driver (in the compartment jutting out of the superstructure), commander, gunner—using an Sfl. Zf 1a sight—and two loaders, something of a squeeze. (Fat yankey/ WikiCommons/CC BY-SA 2.5)

Sturmtiger 19 red at the Kubinka Tank Museum, the photograph showing the immense size of the 38 cm rocket launcher on the Tiger chassis. The crew consisted of driver, radio operator, commander/gunner, and two loaders to handle the 376 kg (829 lb), 1.5 m (4 ft 11 in) long rockets. (Alan Wilson/WikiCommons/CC BY-SA 2.0)

Two images of the fighting compartment of the Wespe with a Waffen-SS crew. Above: Note elevation wheel at right of gun—it had a -5° to 42° elevation. Below: The traverse wheel (17° arc of traverse) is at left beside the gunner who is using his Rbl F 36 gunsight. The Wespe carried 32 rounds—in charges and projectiles—and needed an ammo carrier to keep it supplied. There were five crew: driver up front, gunner at left of gun, radio operator behind him (using an FuSpr. f radio), and commander and loader on the right-hand side. (NARA via Digital Archive)

The Grille Ausf H showing the fighting compartment. The commander's seat **A** is on the higher rear area (because the engine is under it), to the left of a container with six projectiles, and behind the gunner (**B**). The driver's seat is at **C**, below the loader's station and seat **D**. The curved bar is part of the structure that could be erected to allow a tarpaulin to cover the delicate parts of the gun mechanism and the crew. Note the perforated plate at back right: above the engine, it allowed warm air to enter the fighting compartment. (via Panzernet.net)

A Grille *Zug/Batterie*—two Ausf Hs with an SdKfz 251/1—one of which is manned and awaiting a fire order near Aprilia, Italy. Note the knocked-out M4A1 Sherman tank in the background. Delivered from February 1943, there were six Grillen in a PzGr sIG *Kompanie* (usually the 10. Kompanie; later it became the 9. after the organizational change that dispensed with the *Flak-Kompanien* of the Panzergrenadier regiments). (NAC)

The Hummel crew in action: the commander with notebook at left and the gunner at station while two men ram the projectile into the breech. The fifth man prepares to insert the charge. These actions would be repeated three or four times a minute. (Bundesarchiv, Bild 101I-219-0586-11/Harschneck/CC-BY-SA 3.0)

chassis of the later form of Grille saw the engine move to the center of the vehicle. Equipped with the sIG 33/2, this became the Ausf K (with the engine in the middle; 180 built). The Grille had a crew of four (driver in hull, gunner, commander and one or two loaders in the fighting compartment, the commander front right near the FuG 16 radio). BMM also built 102 ammo carriers.

The Wespe and Hummel (wasp and bumblebee respectively) first saw action at the battle of Kursk and would be produced in numbers that saw them still in strength at the end of the war (676 Wespe, 705 Hummel). Wespe mounted the light 10.5 cm leFH 18/2 on a PzKpfw I chassis. It had a crew of four or five—commander, driver (in hull), two/three gunners.

The Hummel mounted a 15 cm sFH 18 L/30 heavy howitzer on a PzKpfw IV chassis (schwere Panzerhaubitze auf Geschützwagen III/IV Sf). The Hummel had a crew of five or six (commander, driver, radio operator, and two/three gun crew). During winter canvas top-covers were employed to keep some of the weather out and heat in: the Hummel had cabin heating from the engine.

The crew prepares to fire a Hummel's 15 cm sFH 18/1 as the gunner works on the gunsight. (The Hummel mounted an Rbl F 36 on a ZE 34.) The traversing mechanism allowed a range of 13° left and 15° right. There were six crew: driver, commander, gunner, and three ammunition handlers: the Hummel carried 18 rounds of two-piece ammo. Note the (red-and-white) aiming posts on the back beneath the doors above the exhaust muffler. (GF Collection)

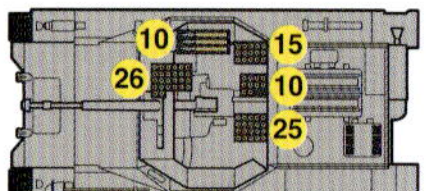

Panzerjäger I

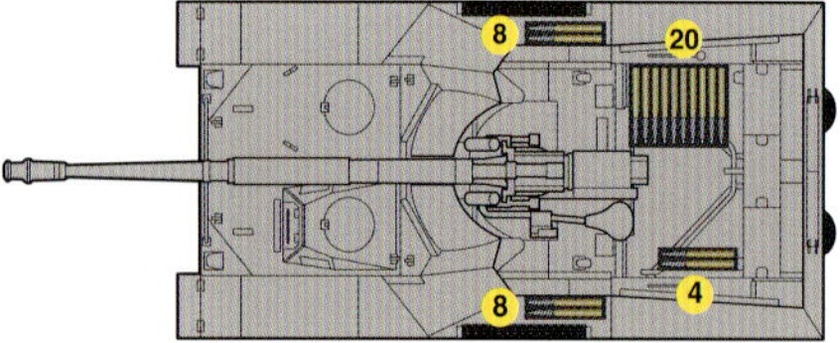

Nashorn/Hornisse

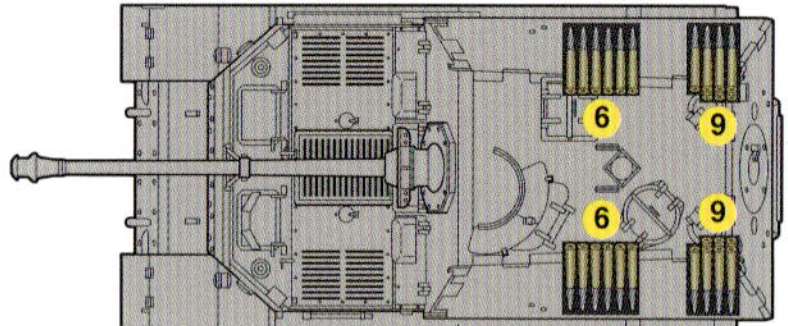

Ferdinand/Elefant

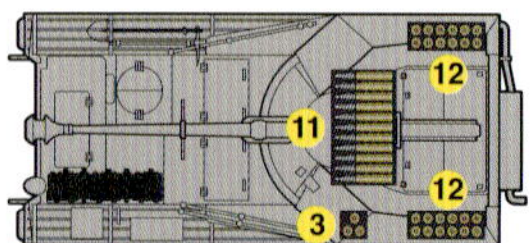

Marder III

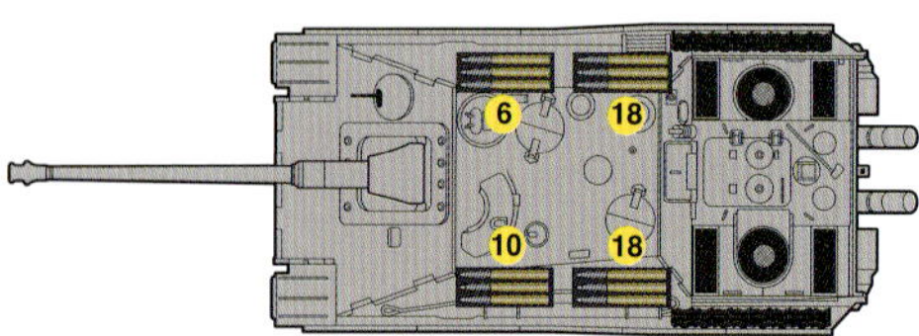

Jagdpanther

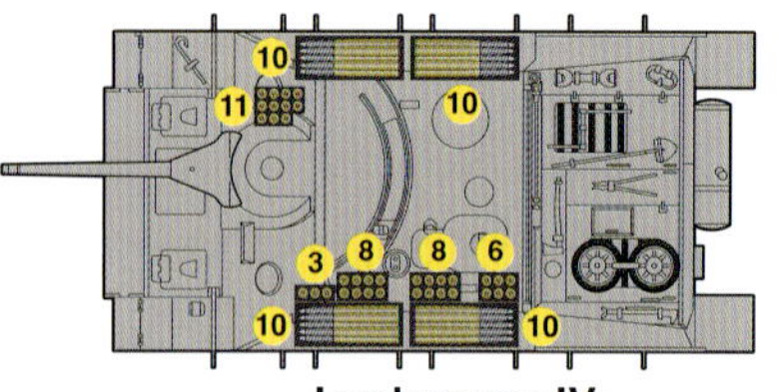

Jagdpanzer IV

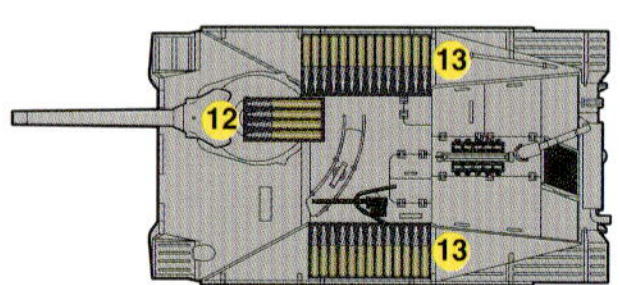

Jagdpanzer 38

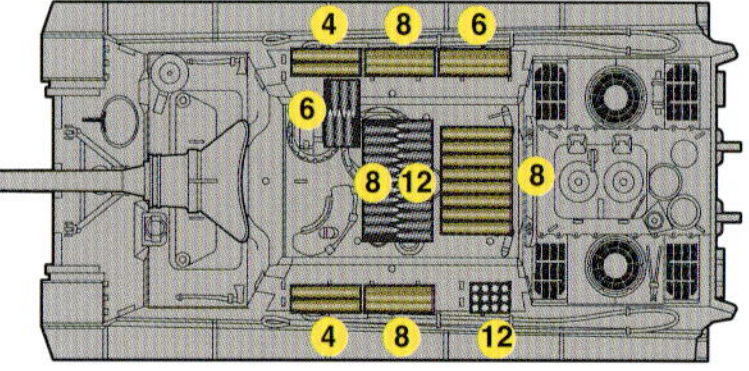

Jagdtiger

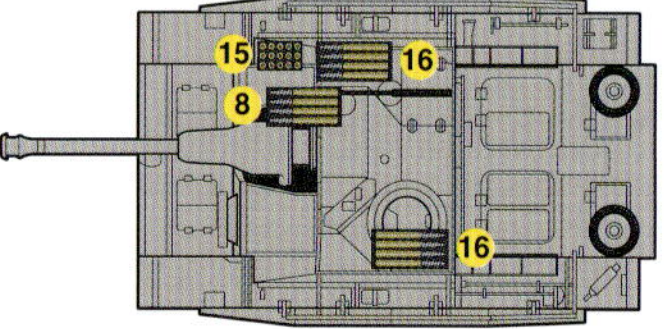

Sturmgeschütz III Ausf G

Ammunition

There was a huge range of ammunition required for the *Sturmgeschütze*, *Panzerjäger*, and *Panzerartillerie* presenting a logistical nightmare. Wherever possible, vehicles (*Munitionsträger*) were used.

All the *Panzerjäger* and *Panzerartillerie* vehicle crews encountered ammunition storage issues: big guns take up a lot of space and that reduces the areas available for ammunition. This was something that the German Army had been thinking about from the 1930s when it looked at the Leichttraktor as a possible starting point for an ammunition carrier. The problem was that they had too much to do and too little time to get everything done: the project fell

Typical stowage for a range of vehicles. (Figures are approximate—individual vehicles differed and often extra ammunition was carried wherever it fitted.)

Panzerjäger I
Main gun: 4.7 cm
Total rounds carried: 86 rounds

Nashorn/Hornisse
Main gun: 8.8 cm
Total rounds carried: 40

Ferdinand/Elefant
Main gun: 8.8 cm
Total rounds carried: 50 (some loose)

Marder III
Main gun: 7.62 cm PaK 36(r)
Total rounds carried: 38

Jagdpanther
Main gun: 8.8 cm
Total rounds carried: 50–60

Jagdpanzer IV
Main gun: 7.5 cm:
Total rounds carried: 76

Jagdpanzer 38
Main gun: 7.5 cm
Total rounds carried: 38–41

Jagdtiger
Main gun: 12.8 cm
Total rounds carried: 38–40 (NB: two-part ammunition)

Sturmgeschütz III Ausf G
Main gun: 7.5 cm
Total rounds carried: 55

The paucity of ammunition stowage in many of the SP guns caused problems—although, as with the tanks, the official ammunition quantities were often exceeded. Here, wicker containers for three shells for this Bison I's 15 cm sIG 33 are visible. The charges were in boxes. Note the Zeiss Rbl F 36 gunsight. Further ammunition would be supplied by trucks or halftracks—some of the crew used the same transport because of the cramped (and cold) fighting compartment. (NARA via Digital Archive)

by the wayside. Next was the PzKpfw I—used in ammunition transport columns during the battles in Poland and the West. Later in the war, a further 122 conversions took place to produce the SdKfz 111 gepanzerte Munitionsschlepper auf Fahrgestell PzKpfw I, mainly for use with SPGs employing the PaK 36(r). It wasn't the best supply vehicle of the war, but it was better than nothing.

The three late-war SP guns used by the *Panzerartillerie* had reduced ammo-carrying ability: the Grille carried about 15 rounds, the Wespe 30, and the Hummel 18. This lack of stowage necessitated efficient resupply. While trucks were often used, dedicated *Munitionsträger* were also produced: 102 of the Munitionspanzer 38(t) (Sf) Grille with a

Several SP guns had their main weapon removed and were used as ammunition carriers. This is a Geschützwagen III/IV für Munition, a late-production Hummel ammunition carrier (early ones had a boxed driver position). The Hummel could only carry 18 full rounds (heavy at 42.9 kg/94.6 lb each)—projectiles plus propellant charges. The ammunition carrier could carry around 85 rounds in their packing cases in stowage racks—the actual number limited by weight. (NARA)

Loader lifts a round for the Nashorn's 8.8 cm PaK 43/1 L/71 gun. It carried four main types of ammunition: Pzgr 39, the main AP round of the war, lethal at 500–1,000 m; Sprgr, the main HE round; Pzgr 40, the best antiarmor round thanks to its tungsten core—but limited in quantity, especially late in the war due to the lack of tungsten; GrHl, a hollow-charge round that was slower than an AP round but was still effective. The size of the shells restricted storage: the roomy Nashorn could only carry 16 in stowage racks and 24 on the floor, so resupply by truck or halftrack was essential. (GF Collection)

capacity of 40 rounds. The crew of the carrier was two: the driver and the commander. The driver was in the hull, the commander in the cargo hold—in charge of radio (FuG 16) and replenishment. 159 Munitions Selbstfahrlafette auf Fahrgestell PzKpfw IIs were built using the Wespe. It could carry 90 rounds and had a crew of two. Then there was the GW III/IV für Munition ammunition carrier: 157 of them were built using the Hummel without a main gun. Other obsolete vehicles were also used to create *Munitionspanzer*: the PzKpfw III and IV—even the StuG III itself.

More successful was the dedicated SdKfz 252 leichter gepanzerter Munitionskraftwagen, 413 of which were built by Demag and Wegmann (June to December 1940) and Deutsche Werke (January to September 1941). Designed to be used by the *StuG-Abteilungen*, it had FuG 15/16 radios and could accommodate—along with the SdAh 32/1 Anhänger (1 achs.) für Munition (7.5 cm) one-axle ammunition trailer—around 200 rounds (the trailer could take 64).

In 1941 production of the SdKfz 252 stopped in favor of the SdKfz 250/6 leichter Munitionspanzerwagen, whose Ausf A carried 70 rounds for the 7.5 cm StuK 37 L/24 gun and Ausf B carried 60 rounds for 7.5 cm StuK 40 L/48 gun.

The official pamphlet *Die Sturmgeschützbatterie* of September 7, 1942, highlighted the important role of the ammunition NCO who led the ammunition trucks. He replenished the battery's ammunition stocks from stores in the rear and ensured that the ammunition was distributed to the battery. By 1944 the organization of a *Munitionsstaffel* in a *Sturmgeschützbrigade* of 10–14 guns was (extras for 14 guns in italics in brackets):

Manpower: NCO in command, 4 (*6*) x drivers, 7 (*11*) x munitions troops, 3 (*5*) also codrivers; 2 in protection MG team

Vehicles: 1 x light cross-country passenger car (probably a VW Typ 82); 3 x 3-tonne open cross-country trucks; 3 (*5*) x single-axle (SdAh 31/1) for 7.5 cm Sturmkanone 40 and 1 x multi-axle 3-tonne ammunition trailers

Setting a shell for the 15 cm sFH 18/1 on a Hummel on the Eastern Front, 1943. Larger weapons use three-part ammunition: charge, projectile, and fuze. Fuzes can be initiated by contact/impact, percussion, time, or (less so in WW2) proximity. The impact fuze was a default setting during manufacture; by using a fuze wrench, as here, the required time was set for the effect required—airburst, proximity, or after what the Germans call *abpraller*, the ricochet technique (see p. 96). (NARA via Digital Archive)

In comparison, the *Munitionsstaffel* for a battery of SP guns using Beute chassis (from KStN 430 of October 31, 1942) was:

Manpower: NCO in command with ammunition NCO, 1 motorcycle messenger, 13 drivers, 24 x munitions troops (12 also codrivers, 3 also engine fitters)

Vehicles: 1 x light passenger car, cross-country, 4 x light ammunition vehicles (SdKfz 250/6), 4 x single-axle (SdAh 31/1) and 8 x single-axle (SdAh 5) ammunition trailers, 8 x trucks

The ammunition resupply for the *Sturmgeschütz* units was provided by the SdKfz 252 with its AhSd 39/1 trailer that could carry 64 7.5 cm rounds. (World War Photos)

Communications

German AFV radio sets were referred to by the abbreviation for radio—*FuG*—followed by a number, or *FuSpr* for the voice transmitting set used in SP artillery vehicles and some armored cars. The table below comes from the U.S. Army's 1945 handbook on German forces and shows the radio sets that were installed in various AFVs:

Vehicle	*Radio*
PzBefWg and BefPz	FuG 8 and FuG 5; or FuG 7 and FuG 5.
Tanks	FuG 5 and FuG 2; or FuG5 only.
Flakpanzer	FuG 5 or FuG 2 only.
Sturmgeschütze (in armored units)	FuG 5 and FuG 2; or FuG 5 only.
Sturmgeschütze (in artillery units)	FuG 8, FuG 16, and FuG 15; or FuG 16 and FuG 15; or FuG 16 only.
Sturmgeschütze (in antitank units)	FuG 8 and FuG 5; or FuG 5 only.
SP *Panzerjäger* (light and medium chassis)	FuG 8 and FuG 5; or FuG 5 only.
SP *Panzerjäger* (heavy chassis)	FuG 8 and FuG 5; or FuG 7 and FuG 5; or FuG 5 and FuG 2.
Panzerartillerie OP vehicles	FuG 8 and FuG 4; or FuG 8, FuG 4, and FuSpr.f
SP heavy infantry gun	FuG 16 only.
Wespe and Hummel	FuSpr.f only.
Lynx (reconnaissance)	FuG 12 and FuSpr.f; or FuSpr.f only.
Armored cars (except eight-wheeled vehicles) and semi-tracked vehicles with armament	FuSpr.f only or FuG 12 and FuSpr.f
Eight-wheeled armored cars	FuG 12 and FuSpr.f; or FuSpr.f only.

The early *Sturmgeschütze* (Ausf A–D) didn't have an intercom. The commander talked to the driver through a speaking tube. There was a radio—as in all German AFVs—that was in the left sponson next to the commander. Initially, in the Ausf A the ultra-shortwave receiver (*Ultrakurzwellen Empfänger*—Ukw.E) was probably a Ukw.E.c1. Ausf B–D were equipped with the FuG 16 SE 10 U system that paired the FuG 16 10-watt Sender h transmitter with the Ukw.E.h receiver. It was attached to a 4W loudspeaker (LSG [Fu] b) that became standard equipment in all models of the StuG, even after a crew intercom—for all but the gunner—was introduced with the Ausf E. Latterly, by early 1943, the gunner, too, received an intercom connection.

The command vehicles had two 2 m rod antennas, each on the left and right sides of the motor separation bulkhead. In the right section of the interior, the loader operated the FuG 16 equipment with its own antenna, while in the left section, the commander operated the FuG15 Ukw.E.h, also with its own antenna. While interaction with the FuG 16 occurred though the onboard intercom box, the FuG 15 receiver could be heard through the loudspeaker. From 1941, earlier StuGs could be converted to the new configuration.

Later StuGs were flexible in their radio setups, with space available in both sponsons which were introduced from the Ausf E. Standard StuG equipment was the FuG 16 transmitter/receiver (with transformers) but other vehicles—particularly those of *Zug* or *Batterie* commanders—carried a FuG 15 as well. The layout of these radios depended on the role of the vehicle. The *Funker* also had a Morse key. The diagram (below) shows the setup for an Ausf G using the FuG 5 and two radios that were issued to vehicles used as *Panzerjäger* or being used by *Panzer-Divisionen*. They were like the FuG 16 and 15 but used different frequencies.

Ausf G radio and intercom setup. Note the loudspeaker that was retained even after the improved communications equipment was introduced. Note, too, the headsets and throat microphones for all four crew linking into the Kasten Pz 24 amplifier—directly for the *Geschützführer* and *Ladeschütze/Funker*; via a Kasten Pz 21 (*Fahrer*) and 25 (*Richtschütze*). The antenna would change depending on the equipment fit: a *Sternantenna* would be necessary for some command vehicles.

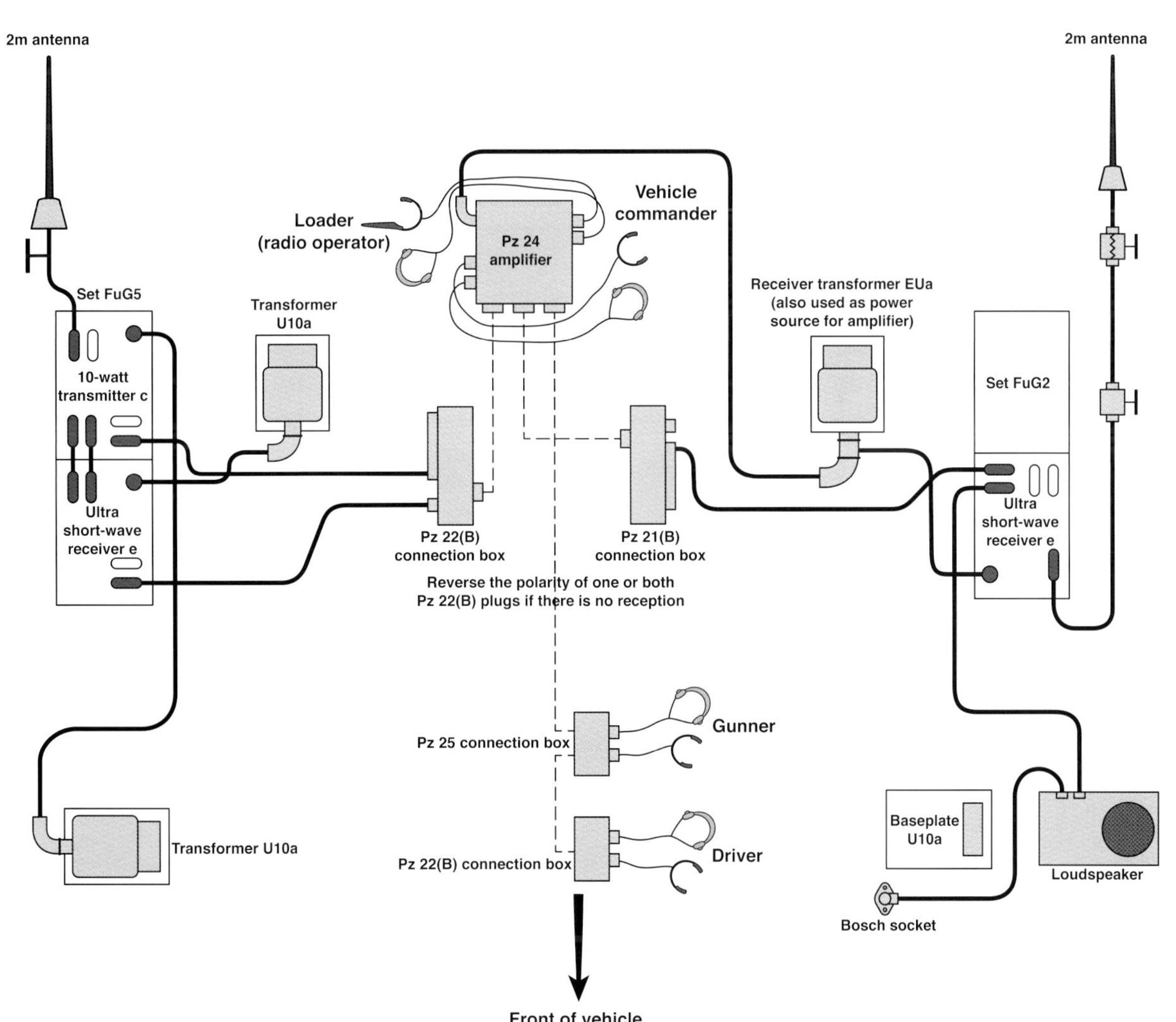

A Wespe of SS-Panzer-Artillerie-Regiment 12, part of 12. SS-Panzer-Division Hitlerjugend, in Normandy in 1944. Note the chicken wire visible on the turret side into which suitable camouflage can be added, in this case foliage. There are four men in the fighting compartment so the chap on the front next to the open driver's hatch with the blanket, late MP 40 with stamped/ribbed magazine housing, and an oak-leaf-patterned smock, is just a passenger. (GF Collection)

Camouflage

At first, all Wehrmacht vehicles were painted in dark gray (*dunkelgrau*). In 1939–40 a secondary color (*dunkelbraun*) was added, although it dropped out of favor and the Wehrmacht reverted to the original scheme. From 1943, *dunkelgrau* was dropped in favor of *dunkelgelb*, with secondary colors of *rotbraun* and *olivgrün*, the latter tending to be the color most often used in the last months of the war. Two more complicated styles of camouflage were often used in the last years of the war: *Hinterhalt-Tarnung* (ambush camouflage) and *Splittermuster* (splinter pattern). Ambush employed extra spots on the three colors: green and brown on yellow, brown and yellow on green, and green and yellow on brown. Splinter used the colors in sharp-edged regular stripes.

Special conditions—the desert of North Africa or the snowy wastes of the Soviet Union—needed different treatment. In November 1941 the Inspectorate issued an order to apply white paint/whitewash to combat vehicles for the duration of the snowy conditions and other vehicles if sufficient paint was available. There was a shortage, so some were partially painted, some were striped, and others only received a coating to the front. If there was no paint available at all, the crew had to improvise: with sheets, chalk, tablecloths, and even paper and

Camouflaging a Jagdpanther in France in 1944. (Bundesarchiv, Bild 101I-721-0397-19/Wagner/CC-BY-SA 3.0)

Another Jagdpanzer 38 showing a rather different paint scheme, a disruptive pattern probably of the same colors (*rotbraun, olivgrün,* and *dunkelgelb*) but complete with eye, grinning mouth, and teeth. The crewmembers are less flamboyant, three wearing the *feldgrau Sturmartillerie* uniform and one in the more conspicuous *Panzer* black. All have *Totenköpfe* on their collars and EK II ribbons on their lapels. Those in *feldgrau* all have General Assault Badges; two have black wound badges and the *Obergefreiter* on the right another unidentifiable award. (Akira Takiguchi)

newsprint. The whitewashing continued as the Germans were better prepared through the winter of 1942/43 until the introduction of the *dunkelgelb* scheme in February.

It's worth noting that colors were standardized but there were variations between manufacturers. Different types of application—brush, rag, spray—also produced different effects.

Ideally, natural camouflage from the location is best and vehicle crews were responsible for this. When static, camouflaging the vehicle was one of the first crew tasks. From mid-war, after the Luftwaffe lost air superiority, AFV crew had to watch out for *Jabos—Jagdbomber* = fighter-bombers—making camouflage even more important. Here, a Finnish unit (there are vehicles and men in the treelines) has done its best to break up outlines and hide the vehicles. Note the StuG 40 Ausf G with *Topfblende* mantlet at right and the cut logs strapped to the sides which, when combined with others, would help fill ditches along with fascines, form a track of sorts over boggy ground, or absorb antitank rounds. (SA-kuva/Finnish Archives)

North Africa required a different camouflage treatment as can be seen on this line of Marder III Ausf Hs newly arrived on Quai Charles Quint, La Goulette, Tunisia. Note the fuel drums, jerrycans of water, tarpaulin roof covers (essential in dust storms), and the *gelbbraun* camouflage color with *graugrün* as the second color (although this is difficult to make out). They would go on to fight with 2./PzJg-Abt 39. (Ian Spring/Pixpast.com)

Opposite, center: A lineup of vehicles to be camouflaged—in front a StuG 40 Ausf G, behind an SdKfz 10/5 armed with a 2 cm FlaK 38—in winter 1944/45. The crew daubs on the paint with whatever brushes they can find, being careful not to obscure their trophy rings. Location and unit are difficult to ascertain although Hungarian Archives suggests Czechoslovakia (*cukrárna/cukráreň* = pastry shop in Czech/Slovak). If that were the case, then it's possible that this is part of PzJg-Abt 95 (3. Gebirgsjäger-Division) that spent the winter in Slovakia. (Fortepan Hungarian Archives)

Opposite, below: This Jagdpanzer IV can be found in the Kubinka Tank Museum. The color scheme represents a crew-painted ambush pattern where the flecks represent dapple, small dots of color highlighted by light shining through leaves or broken structures. The base color would have been *dunkelgelb* with *rotbraun* and *olivgrün* overlaid. (Michel Blinoff)

Below: Jagdpanzer 38(t) in the Kubinka Tank Museum. The photograph highlights the difficult decisions museums have when it comes to repainting—or not—their exhibits. With paint chippings available and a wealth of knowledge to hand, museum colors may look garish on occasion but are usually as accurate as can be expected. There were no set patterns for vehicles and there were sanctioned color schemes. How they were applied was dependent on the surroundings and the imagination of those doing the painting—usually the crew. The colors used are *rotbraun*, *olivgrün*, and *dunkelgelb*. (Michel Blinoff)

With the *Ausfallflagge* (breakdown flag) yellow with a black cross—flying on the radio antenna signifying that help is needed, a scruffy maintenance crewman is checking a manual. The camouflage of this StuG III Ausf E and staff car has been very crudely applied in the field; the early war primary color of *dunkelgrau* has been smeared with *graugrün* (gray green). It blends well with the surroundings. The green symbol on the randomly whitewashed staff car signifies HQ Signal Platoon. The WH (Wehrmacht) on the vehicle was painted on civilian cars before the issue of the official license plate. There is also a flag/pennant reflection by the rear window. (Ian Spring/Pixpast.com)

Crew Duties

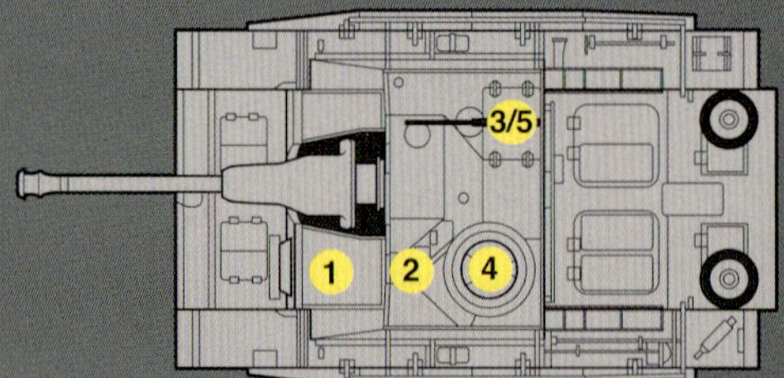

Sturmgeschütz III Ausf G

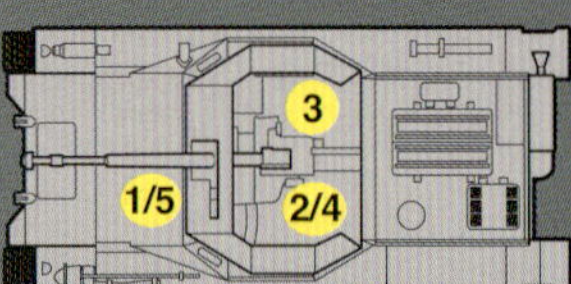

Panzerjäger I

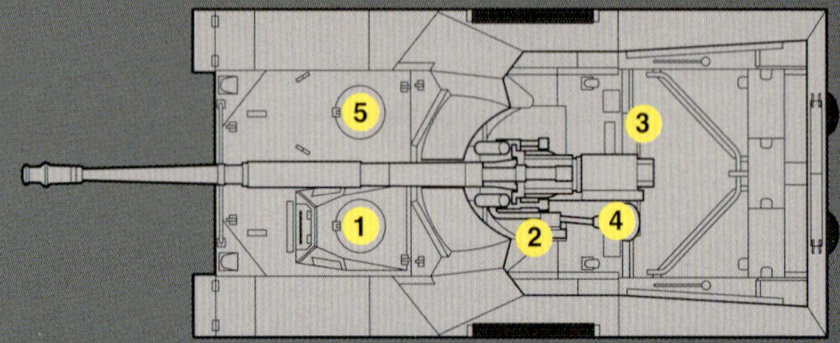

Nashorn/Hornisse

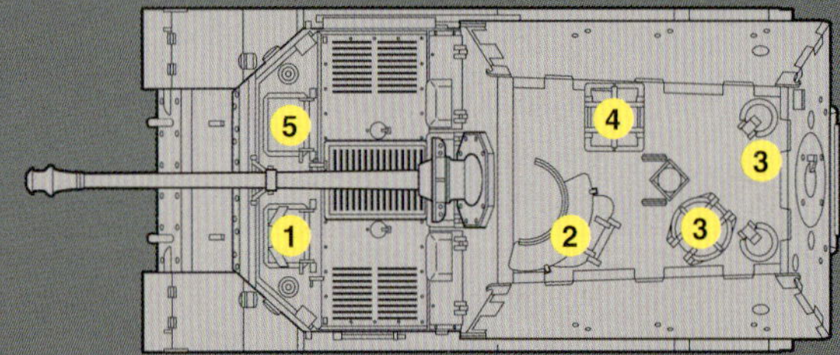

Ferdinand/Elefant

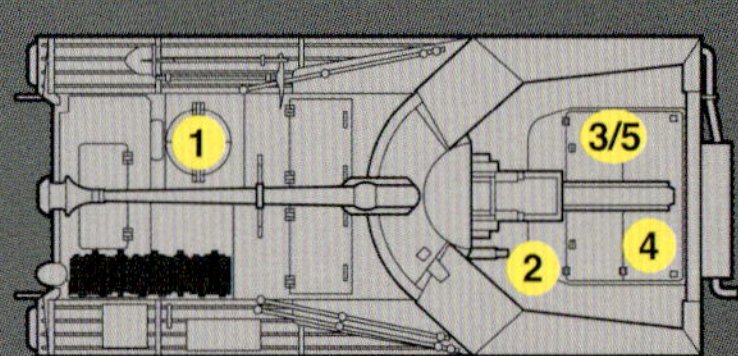

Marder III

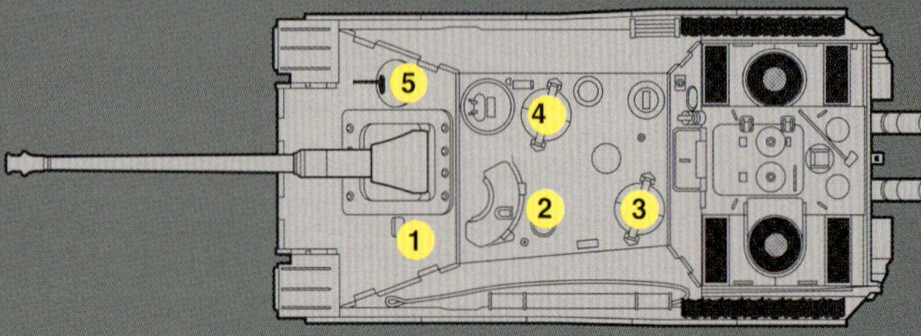

Jagdpanther

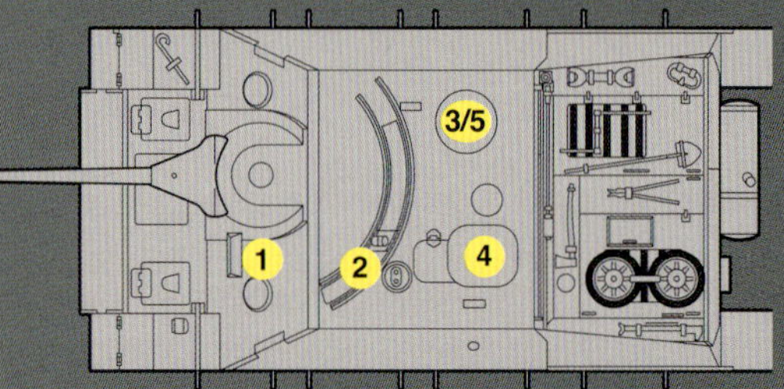

Jagdpanzer IV

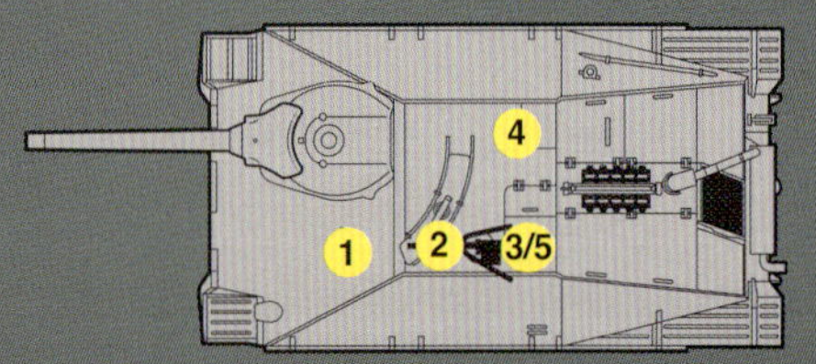

Jagdpanzer 38

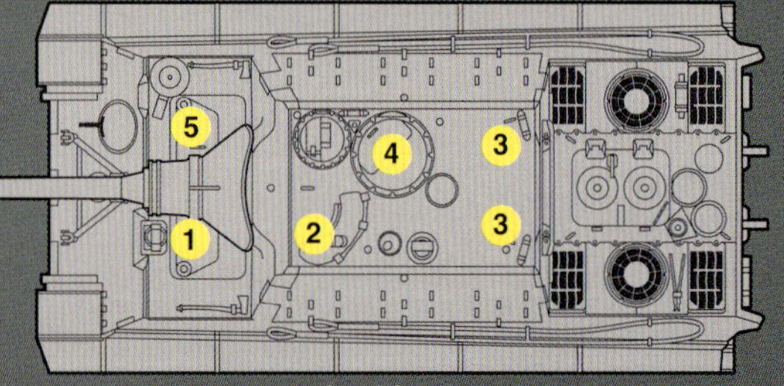

Jagdtiger

Example crew locations for Panzerjäger, SPG, and Sturmgeschütz crew, where:
1 = Driver
2 = Gunner
3 = Loader
4 = Commander
5 = Radio operator (sometimes bow gunner too)

Panzerjäger I
Crew: 3
Driver/radio operator: Front left under armor
Gunner/Commander: Left on fighting platform
Loader: Right on fighting platform

Ferdinand/Elefant
Crew: 6
Driver: Front left under armor (hatch)
Radio operator/bow gunner: Front right under armor (hatch)
Gunner: Left in casemate (sight in roof, no hatch)
Commander: Front right in casemate (hatch/cupola from refit)
Loader: Back left in casemate (hatch)
Assistant loader: Back right in casemate (large circular hatch on backplate)

Jagdpanther
Crew: 5
Driver: Front left of hull
Radio operator/machine gunner: Front right of hull
Commander: Right side (hatch and, later, cupola)
Gunner: Left side (sight in roof, no hatch)
Loader: Left rear (hatch)

Jagdpanzer 38
Crew: 4
Driver: Front left of hull
Gunner: Left side (sight in roof, no hatch)
Loader/radio operator: Left rear (hatch); fired remote-controlled roof-mounted MG
Commander: Back right (hatch)

Sturmgeschütz III Ausf G
Crew: 4
Driver: Front left of hull (hatch)
Gunner: Left side (sight in roof, no hatch)
Loader/radio operator: Right side (hatch); fired roof-mounted MG and later remote-controlled version
Commander: Back left (hatch with cupola)

Nashorn/Hornisse
Crew: 5
Driver: Front left under armor (hatch)
Radio operator: Front right under armor (hatch)
Gunner: Left front of firing platform
Loader: Right of firing platform
Commander: Back left of firing platform

Marder III
Crew: 4
Driver: On right side of vehicle under armor (hatch)
Gunner: On left of firing platform
Loader/radio operator: On right of firing platform
Commander: Rear of firing platform (or out of vehicle)

Jagdpanzer IV
Crew: 4
Driver: Front left of hull
Commander: Left rear (hatch)
Gunner: Left side (sight in roof, no hatch)
Loader/radio operator: Right side (hatch)

Jagdtiger
Crew: 6
Driver: Front left of hull (hatch)
Radio operator/bow gunner: Front right of hull (hatch)
Commander: Right side (hatch with cupola)
Gunner: Left side (sight in roof, no hatch)
Loader and assistant loader: Back (hatch in rear of casemate)

Cutaway Finnish *Sturmi* at the Parola Armor Museum. Used for training, it provides a graphic view of the cramped conditions on the left side of the fighting compartment where driver, gunner, and commander jostled for room. The gunner in this photo has hold of the elevation wheel. (Parola Armor Museum)

Higher Command

a) *Batterie* OC

The *Batterie* OC is responsible for liaison with the infantry commander for a joint attack, gives the necessary orders to his units, uses his 2IC or a liaison NCO to communicate with the infantry while maintaining close contact with his units near the front. His direct involvement in the battle should only take place if forced upon him. He is also responsible for ensuring his units are suitably provided with ammunition, fuel, and provisions.

b) *Batterie* 2IC

The adjutant or executive officer does what the commander needs him to, often as leader of the supply squadron. If the *Batterie* OC is with his unit, the 2IC will be with the infantry commander. The 2IC oversees the *Batterie-Stab* unit.

A view of the Parola Ausf G's interior. Note radios on loader's side: at left a 30W Sender a medium-frequency transmitter and at right a Mittelwellenempfänger c medium-wave receiver. This radio type was used by *Panzer* units to communicate with their higher headquarters. In the foreground is the gunner's seat (the commander's has been removed for photography), the big wheel handling elevation. Gunner's sight is obvious top center. (Parola Armor Museum)

c) *Zug* leader
Has more importance if the *Zug* is deployed independently, when he needs to liaise with the infantry leader. Responsible for deployment of his platoon, reconnaissance, identification of targets, and selection of the starting position for the assault. During the engagement, he leads his *Zug* as directed by superiors, indicating targets by radio or directional shots from his gun. He must maintain close contact with the infantry so he can identify new targets to his unit quickly—particularly those pointed out by the infantry commander. He's responsible for replenishment of supplies and personnel, for keeping his *Batterie* OC in touch with the situation.

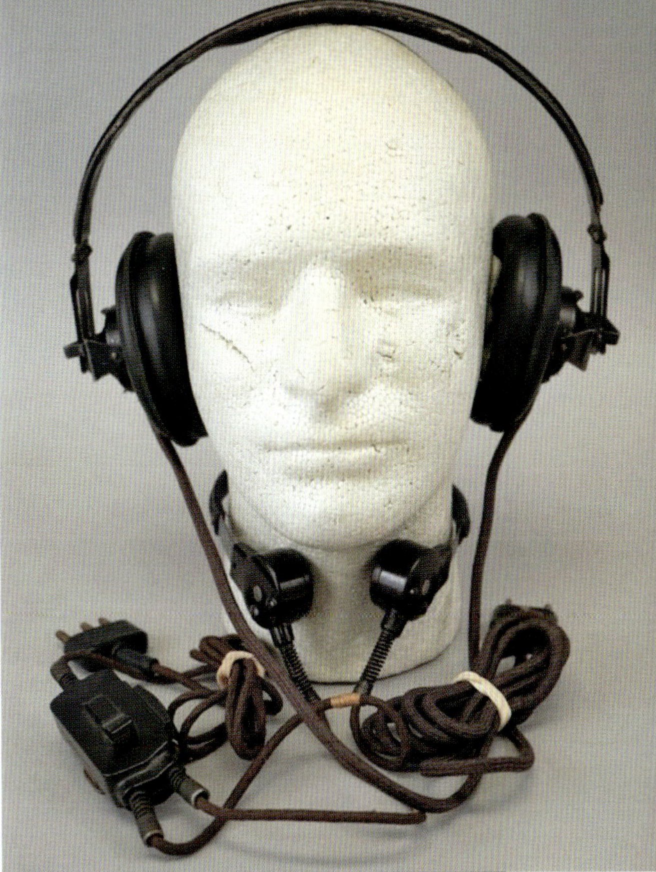

Model B headset and throat microphone for use in armored vehicles: note Bakelite earphones with rubber earcups, leather-wrapped metal headband, and connection cord. Bakelite microphones attached to leather-wrapped neck set with electrical connection cord and activation switch in housing. (www.themarshalsbaton.com)

Gun Crew

The interior of any AFV is usually cramped, smelly, and uncomfortable. The *Sturmgeschütz* was more cramped than most. Observation was also always a problem for AFV crew, particularly in a firefight when buttoned up. In StuGs, all-round observation was always a problem because of the nature of a turretless vehicle. Even when the commander's position was given a revolving cupola that worked (lack of ball bearings meant that many were fixed in place), there were enough blind spots to ensure that all the training information insisted that a StuG shouldn't get involved with enemy infantry unless it had its own supporting ground troops. The gun commander was responsible for monitoring the close protection of the gun—especially to the rear—with the driver looking to the front and left, the loader to the right, and the gunner looking to the front when firing and elsewhere as necessary. "Be vigilant and have eyes everywhere," the manuals advise, "not only to spot the tanks in front but at every angle: right, left, even backward."

***Geschützführer* (Gun Commander)**
The commander sat at the back left of the vehicle on a spring-loaded seat that could be raised to allow him to look out of the top of the superstructure. He had a scissors periscope, but he could only use it if his hatch was open.

His role was to lead his gun according to his mission, attacking those targets he had been ordered to and choosing other targets as the exigencies of the situation required. He

Above left: Großdeutschland StuG 40 Ausf G commander wearing his *feldgrau* uniform with cuff-title and standing in his cupola—not a position to take up when the enemy was about. The tank commander was always a favorite target. Note the Scherenfernrohr 14Z peeping above the cupola and the metal shot deflector. A January 1944 photo. (Bundesarchiv Bild 101I-0429-35A/Scheerer/CC-BY-SA 3.0)

Above right: Lineup of damaged StuGs led by an Ausf G. Note the deflector added to the area below the commander's cupola: they were installed on some vehicles from October 1943—and all by February 1944. Those that didn't get steel ones used concrete instead. The area had proved to be a shot trap. Note too the *Topfblende* or *gegossener Rohrwiegenpanzerung* (cast tube cradle armor) mantlet. This is an early one without the telltale hole for a coaxial MG. The L/48 7.5 cm main gun had an excellent armor-piercing record which helped the *Langrohr* StuGs become such efficient tank destroyers. (GF Collection)

Opposite: S/Sgt Börje Brotell near Vyborg on July 7, 1944. He's inside an Ausf G (with round commander's cupola) using his *Scherenfernrohr*. Note Dfh b headphones and throat microphone, the eyepiece of the telescope, his Finnish sidecap with national blue-and-white cockade, and leather jacket. Börje's *Sturmi* was nicknamed "Bubi" and he's credited with destroying 11 enemy tanks during the battle of Tali-Ihantala, five on the first day (June 25, 1944). (SA-kuva/Finnish Archives)

found the best firing positions for his vehicle, ensured that his gunner was aware of the targets, checked aiming, and if he had to, aimed the gun himself. His training promoted *Auftragstaktik*: he was told his commander's intention—what the mission was—but not the specifics of how to do it. That was up to him.

Amongst his responsibilities, he also monitored radio traffic and gave the gun loader, the *Ladekanonier*—who was also the radio operator—radio messages to be sent, so that he could keep his *Zug* leader aware of how the mission was proceeding and ammunition levels. It was emphasized in training how important it was that every commander understood the need to report much and well. He was on the front line, he was the eyes of his commanding officer. He had to be eager to report, but his reports had to be militarily accurate and reliable. He was taught always to try to report the essential according to the intent of the mission—to keep in mind the questions: what must the leadership know? What is of decisive importance for the success of the battle?

However, additionally he also had to report if nothing had changed and that nothing was happening because that too could be important. A commander, he was told, trained his radioman to understand his shouted words and turn them into coherent messages. This was not as straightforward as it sounds because the Soviets were good at radio intercepting and listening in to indiscreet messaging. Bruno Friesen remembered:

> For us, radio silence was not mandatory. Urgent messages could be transmitted within the four-Panzer unit. However, our report to the Company C.O. would have to be couched in language unintelligible to any listening Soviets … Our predicament would keep us from sending anything like a basic report, structured in accordance with the answers to five questions prompted by the a e i o u series where a stood for *wann?* (when?); e, for *wer?* (who?); i, for *wie?* (how?); o, for *wo?* (where?); and u, for was *tue ich weiter?* (what will I do next?).

The *Geschützführer* had to be able to operate the radio himself. In many of the communications setups in the StuG, the radios were split so that he had responsibility for a command network. The *Geschützführer* had to be able to talk to his platoon commander or battery commander, avoiding mistakes and saving valuable time.

In combat, the *Geschützführer* needed to know about the tanks he'd be fighting: their vulnerabilities, specifications, and characteristics. He was taught not to open fire too early from favorable positions. Unless very well sited, effective shooting distances were generally not more than 1,000 m. The StuG crews were artillery-taught and so used bracketing to adjust their fire. Success in combat is often determined by who shoots first. The StuG crew had to be able to work quickly but calmly and with confidence in their weapon and training. The enemy's technical advantage—in particular, a turning turret—could be beaten by "smooth cooperation and intrepid operation."

Remote-controlled Machine Gun

from *Intelligence Bulletin*, May 1945

The Germans are equipping tank destroyers and assault guns with an indirect-laying and indirect-aiming device so that the personnel of these heavy armored vehicles can put up an improved defense against close-in attacks without exposing themselves. The new device consists of a standard light machine gun, the MG 34, mounted on top of the armored fighting compartment. This remote-controlled gun differs from previous forms of superstructure-mounted machine guns in that each of the conventional types must be operated by a man standing with his head and shoulders exposed above an open hatch. Although some protection is afforded by a folding shield which faces forward, the conventional mounts permit forward fire only. This new type of mount is designed to give protection against attack from sides and rear and to supplement the fire of the bow gun.

The remote-controlled MG had a gunshield that protected the mechanism and had space for a standard 50-round drum magazine. It could be aimed and fired while the gunner—the *Ladekanonier* or loader—remained inside the fighting compartment. He controlled the traverse with one hand; with the other, the elevation. He used a periscope to aim. While he could fire from under cover, the drawback was that he had to open a hatch to reload. (U.S. Army)

Over and over it was drummed into the StuG crew: the decisive factors are your spirit and skill and the performance of your gun. "Russian tanks are no opponents for us! If the situation allows, wait and let them run up!"

Another key element in AFV fighting is availability and use of ammunition. The StuGs didn't carry as much as the tanks—there just wasn't room. While there are reports of crew piling in extra rounds—even sitting on them—using the right round for the right job was essential. The key points from the manual were:

- Save armor-piercing shells for their real purpose.
- PzGr 39 can be used at all distances; PzGr 40 has greater penetrating power but should only be used at close distances. Do not use over 800 m if possible.
- Hollow charge: good penetrating power and blasting effect against living targets but it has a longer flight time and larger dispersion.
- Smoke shell: use as directing shots for signaling, for blinding and setting houses on fire.
- HE shell: shoot with delayed fuze if possible. Good effect against living targets in areas or also for bunker busting. In case of emergency, it can also be used against tanks.

Richtschütze (Gunner)

The gunner was the second-in-command of the StuG. He was responsible for getting the StuG combat ready, ensuring the optics were right, and that the fixed locks—if they were being used—were taken off the gun properly—getting this wrong could misalign or even damage parts of the gun. The gunner received initial target instructions and firing orders from the gun commander but was able to attack the target given to him independently, thus freeing up the platoon or battery commander for further target reconnaissance and leadership tasks.

The gunner needed to remember that there was a cap for protecting the barrel—there should be five of them onboard. There was a specific warning about firing in the cold: if the gun barrel was frozen, explosive shells shouldn't be used. In case of hollow-charge rounds, the muzzle cap always had to be removed first. The gunner was also responsible for igniting the 90-second fuze on the demolition charge. If the vehicle had one, it was stored under his seat to destroy a vehicle that couldn't be retrieved or repaired.

Sighting

The reticle on the sight provided an aiming point (center of screen) and allowed the user to calculate distance using the length of the image on the reticle. Assessing the size of the image on the reticle provided the gunner with the numbers he needed to give range: distance = actual width x 1000 divided by width in mils on the sight. This calculation quickly became second nature to gunners. (For a more detailed analysis see panzerworld.com/german-armor-optics.)

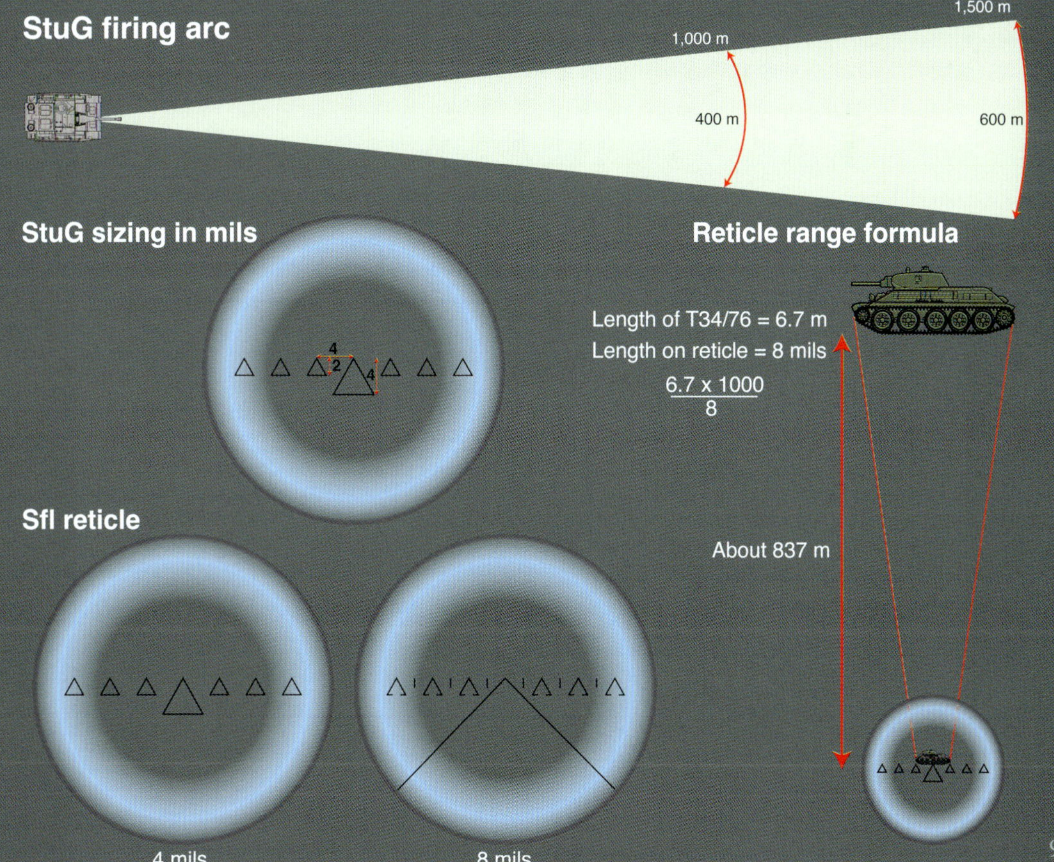

Abpraller (Ricochet/Rebounds)

A standard artillery technique practiced from the early days of cannon, ricochets allowed shells to airburst, which was useful against unprotected targets or those that had adequate frontal—but lacked suitable overhead—protection. It's an unreliable science as a variety of factors affect the outcome: the nature of the terrain, the angle of impact, and of course, the charge itself. The subject was discussed in the U.S. Army's *Field Artillery Journal* (September 1943, p. 697):

> Considerable progress has been made by German artillery in the use of ricochet fire. It is recognized as being useful, effective, and not mysterious. Although it cannot be used in every case, the possibility should always be examined. Our own investigations have borne great fruit, and as our doctrine develops it is interesting to see what the Germans have to say.
>
> "Investigate the possibility of using ricochets. The decisive factor is the angle of impact on the terrain, not the angle of fall. Angles of impact up to 15° can be expected to result in ricochets; and even beyond that (up to 20°) ricochets are possible. In many instances it will be necessary to resort to practical trial. We have found ricochets entirely practicable at angles of impact of 30° and greater. ... [However] a projectile may be deflected from its plane of fire when it ricochets.
>
> "Adjust with non-delay fuze, obtaining a bracket conforming to the depth of the target. After a shot has been placed within the target, change to fire for effect with delay-action fuze at the range diminished by 50 meters. Reducing the limits of the zone for fire for effect compensates for the projectile's additional travel, between its point of impact and point of burst. If ricochet fire for effect were conducted through the bracket established by a super-quick-fuzed projectile, part of the effect would be 'over' and the near edge of the target would remain unscathed.
>
> "When firing ricochets, a change in charge calls for renewed bracketing."

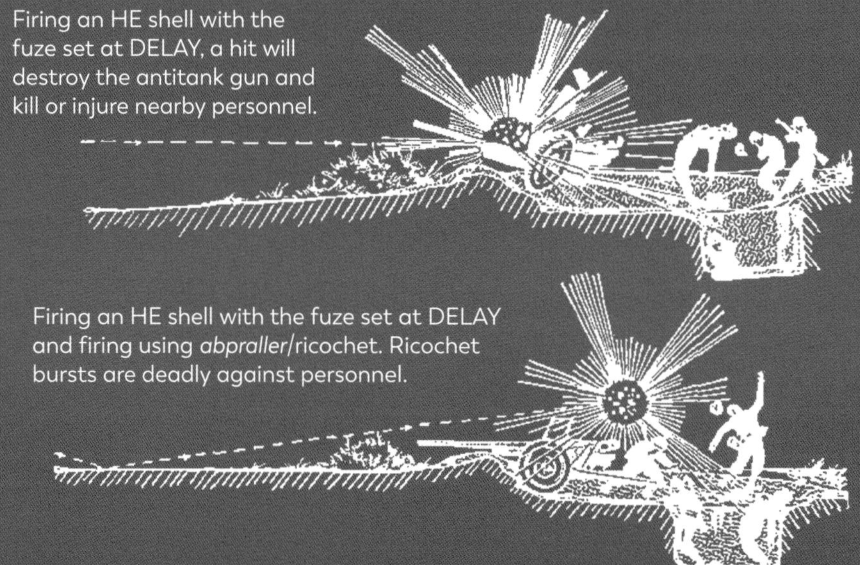

Firing an HE shell with the fuze set at DELAY, a hit will destroy the antitank gun and kill or injure nearby personnel.

Firing an HE shell with the fuze set at DELAY and firing using *abpraller*/ricochet. Ricochet bursts are deadly against personnel.

Looking across from the loader's position, here the commander (at left) is using his *Scherenfernrohr*. The gunner—pipe in hand—rests on the elevation wheel, the hood of his sight by the peak of his *Einheitsfeldmütze*. (GF Collection)

Firing the Main Gun

The commander's first order identifies the type of round, followed by target: for example "*Aufschlag*! (*Mit Verzögerung*),"—point detonation with delay—"*Panzergranate*" (armor-piercing) or "*Nebelgranate*" (smoke round); "MG on the left edge of the bush! 500!" The loader chooses the round required and inserts it into the chamber with both hands. Then he pushes it tight with a closed left fist and the breech closes automatically. Then he presses the electrical safety switch button to "*Feuer*" (fire) with his left thumb and reports "*Geladen*" (loaded).

The gunner has roughly adjusted the cross level, set the distance and type of projectile ordered by the commander, and searched for the target, fine-tuning the cross level as he picks the target up.

After "*Feuer!*" from the commander he presses the trigger, activating the electrical firing. When firing, he remains with his eye on the periscopic gunsight to observe the shot.

The commander also observes the shot through his telescope and orders any improvement that may become necessary. After the new command, the gunner continues firing independently, making the side correction after his own observation, adjusting the distance correction according to the commander's specifications.

So, the gunner corrects horizontally, the commander vertically.

The loader reloads after each shot, sets the safety switch to "fire" and constantly monitors the barrel return indicator. When this reaches the mark "fire break," in peacetime, he would report "*Feuerpause*" (pause in firing). In wartime, firing must continue if the vehicle can't make for cover and needs to keep firing. As soon as possible afterward, all fire activity needs to be interrupted.

At the end of the engagement the commander will order "*Halt!*" and then "*Entladen*" (unload). The loader then switches the electrical safety switch to "safe" and opens the breech with his left hand, removes the round, puts it in the ammunition box, and reports "*Entladen! Rohr leer!*" (Unloaded! Barrel empty!).

The loader in Börje Brotell's Ps.531-10 "Bubi" is Armas Launikko, seen in position with a round ready to load. Note the other rounds in the rack by his shoulder and the cover on the Ukw. E h radio—a radio receiver used almost exclusively in the *Sturmgeschütz*—in conjunction with the 10W Sender h. They were used for communication between *Kompanie* and *Abteilung Stab*. (SA-kuva/Finnish Archives)

The choice of ammunition was dependent on the target: MG or HE for infantry; HESH (high-explosive squash head) for strongpoints; AP for AFVs. While most of the targeting was flat and direct, there were also different techniques used—airburst, ricochet/rebound, etc. The decision to mount weapons in fixed mounts rather than turrets reduced the flexibility that tanks had but did mean bigger guns. The problem was that these were often unwieldy (the L/70 of the Jagdpanzer IV, for example) and very sensitive. Gunners had to be sure that the long barrels were locked down when in transit because even the slightest knock or significant vibration could mean resighting at best or a complete loss of the ability to traverse and elevate which essentially rendered the vehicle out of action.

***Ladekanonier/Funker* (Loader/Radio Operator)**

The loader sets the fuzes, monitors the condition and amount of ammunition, and resolves, as far as possible, any unusual incidents. He's the gofer of the crew, usually the least-experienced member who will take over as a gunner when he is sufficiently trained. As a radio operator, he maintains and operates the radio.

The loader is also responsible for firing a roof-mounted MG (see p. 94). From December 1942, the StuG 40 Ausf G could mount an MG 34 and shield (the shield was retrofitted to some vehicles). From 1944, StuGs received coaxial MGs and in mid-1944 a remote-controlled MG that was added to the roof. It was mounted on a hollow column base and had a 50-round magazine that had to be reloaded externally. The loader had to be ready to engage any infantry that threatened his vehicle with hand grenades, the roof-mounted MG, or SMG.

The loader should arrange the ammunition as determined by the commander. Armor-piercing shells should always be at hand. Also important was that only armor-piercing shells should be stored in the ammunition box near the commander: no hollow-charge or HE shells here because of the danger of explosion.

The loader needed to be aware of what was going on around him, the names of the platoon and assault gun commanders around him, and the structure of his unit so that he could act as radio operator in all events and incidents.

Sturmgeschützfahrer (Driver)

The driver's visibility was quite poor. He had a fixed vision slit to left and a visor in the superstructure to the front, but if the vehicle were under fire, then this had to be closed, and his forward view would have had to come from a twin periscope. The driver's role in the *Sturmgeschütz* was extremely important. The main gun had only a small amount of traverse and it was essential that the driver positioned the vehicle well.

All the vehicles discussed in this book had their own idiosyncrasies and problems. Bruno Friesen was both a PzKpfw IV and, later, PzKpfw IV/70 gunner but he had started life as a driver. In his autobiography he discusses the problems surrounding driving the Jagdpanzer IV that was known for its easily overstressed transmission—caused by a combination of factors including being nose-heavy. As ever, the key to using the Jagdpanzer IV's manual gearbox, with its six forward gears and one reverse, was speed. The vehicle had to accelerate to the top of the gear's range before it could be shifted higher. As the speed—and gear—increased, so did the size of the turning circle (from c. 6 m in first gear to 72 m in sixth). To turn more tightly, as was often needed in combat, one track had to be braked fully but that, as Bruno says, "invited transmission damage."

One of the easiest ways to damage the transmission was when the *Jagdpanzer* was employed to recover a stuck or damaged vehicle. Often involving the pulling power of two *Jagdpanzers*, this was considerably more difficult than towing.

Bruno also discussed the disadvantages of the *Ostketten*: their added weight (a 99-link track weighed almost twice as much with *Ostketten*); their width stopped them crossing military bridges on flatcars, and they were prone to shed when the vehicle turned tightly.

Starting the StuG could be by electrical ignition system or manual inertia starter—the latter being preferred. It was advised not to use the electric starter immediately after refueling for fear of danger of explosion. The driver was even more important in the StuG than in a tank because he had to turn the vehicle before it could engage targets. If the commander hadn't spotted a threat such as an antitank gun or tank, the driver was expected to take independent action.

Driver's station in the Parola Ausf G showing the controls at right, steering columns, and vision slit. When in combat that would be closed and the driver would have to use a periscope. The light from the open inspection/escape hatch shows how much of a squeeze it would be to use. (Parola Armor Museum)

Life in the Line

Finnish StuG 40 Ausf G near Vuosalmi, a village on the Karelian Isthmus, Finland, July 1944. Its Finnish crew are with a group carrying out routine maintenance—a regular necessity. A folding toolbox, sledgehammer, a 20-liter jerrycan, and crowbar are to be seen along with other bits and pieces. The cut timber on the side would be used for traction on softer ground, or filling ditches. The man with his foot on the wooden barrel wears leather m/36 tank crew trousers and the one crouching the gray tank crew overalls. Three others wear cotton/woolen variations of the m/36 summer tunics with softer collars and m/34 breeches. They wear m/36 field cap, based on the *Jaeger* cap or the visorless m/22. (SA-Kuva/Finnish National Archives)

Food and drink are always central to a soldier's life, and the quality and amount available was often an issue—particularly when the advance outstripped the supply lines or in retreat with the Red Army snapping at your heels. Ration packs—as with every army—were monotonous if nutritious. Parcels from home were always awaited expectantly. And when the going got tough, AFV crews kept themselves going with Scho-Ka-Kola (Schokolade Kaffee Kolanuss), launched in 1936 for the Berlin Summer Olympics. A brand of chocolate with a strong caffeine and Kola nut mix, it was included in ration packs and used to extend wakefulness. An early energy drink! (Fotocollectie Spaarnestad Underwerpe/ Nationaalarchief; Jan Wellen/WikiCommons CC BY-SA 3.0)

Barrel cleaning, Eastern Front, 1944. An important task, the angle of the barrel dictates the effort that goes into cleaning it. They are scoured carefully to remove gases and residue after firing, using rods, bore brush, and a solid rubber pad as well as rags. The muzzle brake or recoil compensator was designed to redirect a portion of propellant gasses to reduce recoil and muzzle rise. (Fotocollectie Spaarnestad Underwerpe/Nationaalarchief)

A Großdeutschland StuG crew makes use of the gun barrel to erect their *Zeltbahn* tent. Each soldier had a waterproof triangular shelter/cape, 203 cm x 203 cm x 240 cm with a dark-green *Splitter* (Splinter) pattern on one side and a lighter one on the other. Each side had 31 buttons with a shared buttonhole, and each corner a reinforced peg hole, two having a short length of sturdy string. In the center, a double-flapped opening allowed it to be used as a rain cape. By joining a number together—in this case four—you can make a pup tent. Each soldier had one, along with three alu pegs and a three-part tent pole, as part of his assault equipment. (GF Collection)

And after a hard day's work what better than a river to cool you down. (World War photos)

Notek *Kraftfahrzeug-Nachtmarschgerät* (Motor Vehicle Night-driving Device)

All military vehicles need to be able to drive at night, often in convoy, preferably without advertising their position to the enemy. German AFVs and motor vehicles used a system developed by the Nova-Technik GmbH, Munich and introduced just before the war (although not all vehicles had them when Poland was attacked). This consisted of (a) front light, always placed on the left, that used a mirror to shine reflected light onto a c. 80 ft stretch of road in front of the vehicle; (b) box at the rear (again always placed on the left) that provided convoy lights; (c) a dashboard controller; and (d) a two-level red light could also be attached at the right rear of the vehicle.

The front light had three settings: dim, medium, and full. Visibility of these from the air ranged from below 2,000 ft on the dim setting to below 6,400 ft on the brightest. The box at the rear could be allowed to illuminate the license plate, had a shutter that allowed either the convoy lights or brake lights to be visible, some devices having a hole that allowed the red brake light to be dimly visible when the convoy light shutter was down. This could be reinforced by the use of the extra red light at right rear.

Later in the war other options were available (but not always used; the Notek system carried on being used till war's end): tubular taillights that gave off a blue light and Bosch shuttered headlights.

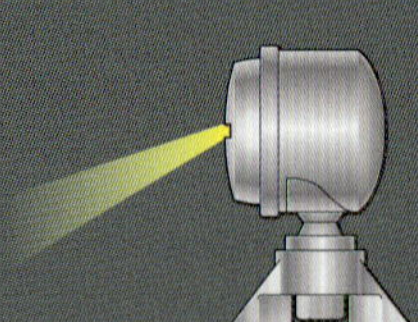

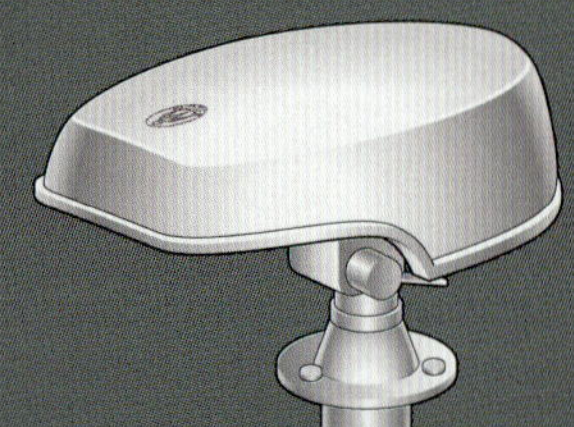
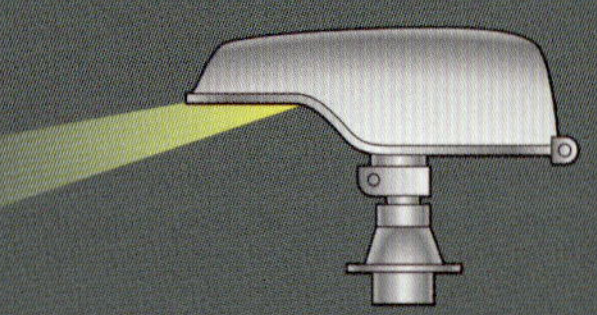

Notek left taillight (early production vehicles)

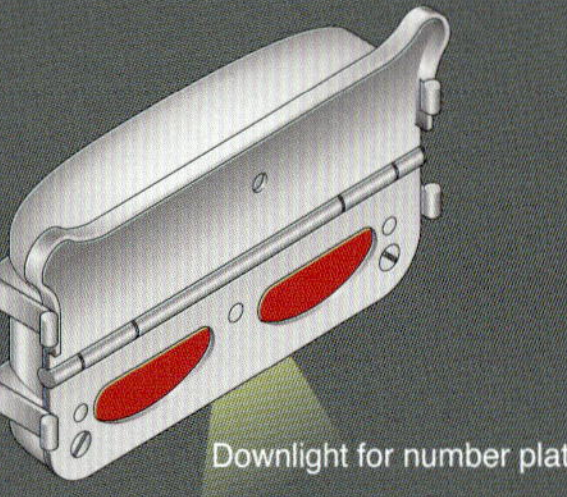

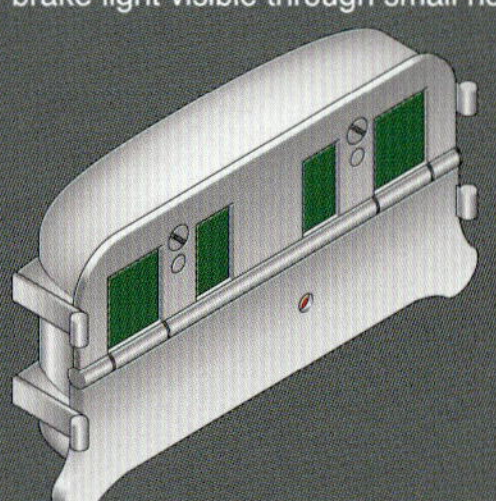

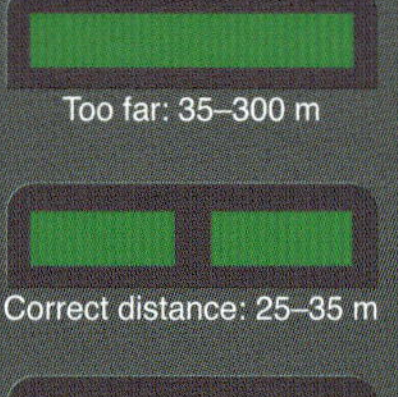

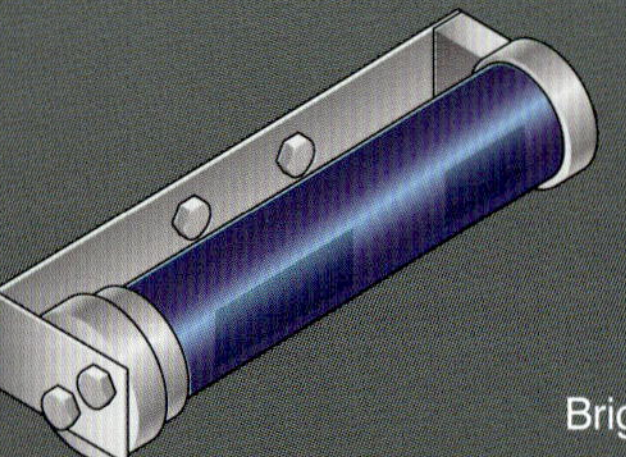

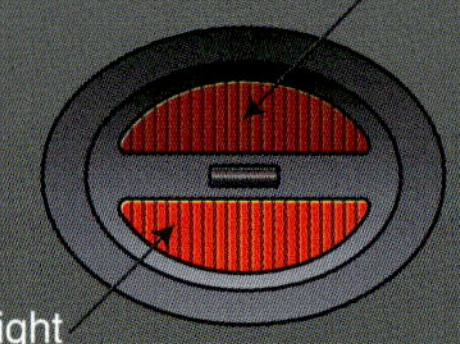

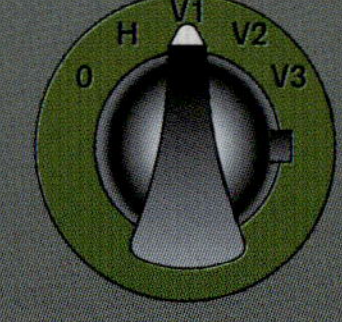

Position	Headlamp	Rear light
O	Off	Off
H	Off	On
V1	Low	On
V2	Medium	On
V3	Full	On

| The Units

The number of *Sturmgeschütz* units, their titles, and weaponry changed considerably over the war. Slow to be appreciated and the subject of continued debate between *Artillerie* and *Panzer* arms of service as to who should control them, they proved immediately successful in small numbers in France and production numbers increased quickly.

The first formation was the *Sturmartillerie Batterie*, each of three *Züge* (platoons) of two StuGs, giving a total of six vehicles. There were also ammunition carriers—SdKfz 250s with SdAh 32/1 trailers.

The success of the *Sturmgeschütze* in the West led to an immediate change of numbers and organization. *Sturmartillerie-Abteilungen*—each with three *Batterien* of two StuGs, giving a total of 18—were created. In early 1941 they were renamed *Sturmgeschütz-Abteilungen*: in total around 60 *StuG-Abteilungen* were set up during the war. Shortly after the name change, the *Abteilungen* gained an extra StuG for the commander (hitherto, he had usually used an SdKfz 253 or 250).

Further reorganizations took place in 1942: first when the number of vehicles in each *Zug* increased to three (giving 2 x *Batterien* each of 3 x *Züge* = 27 + 1 (Abt CO) = 28 StuGs. Later in the year that number increased to 31 as the command troop of the *Abteilung* gained extra vehicles. From February 25, 1944, many of these *Abteilungen* became *Brigaden* without any change to their size and while retaining the same numerical designation.

StuG Nr 203 of 2./StuG-Abt 184, one of the first vehicles of the relief column to enter Kholm (Cholm in German) on May 5, 1942. 2. Batterie was commanded by Oberleutnant der Reserve Richard Hohenhausen whose valor in breaking the 105-day siege earned him the Knight's Cross. As far as its number is concerned, the German AFV numbering system can be misleading. At first (see photo on p. 105), the StuGs used a double-digit system, later changing to the three digits used by the *Panzer-Divisionen*. This somewhat naïve three-digit approach (delineating company/platoon/vehicle) held sway for a while but as the Red Army worked out what was happening—and started to use the system to attack command vehicles—other methods were used. Here, 203 could break down to 2 = *Batterie*, 03 = third vehicle in the *Stab*. (Akira Takiguchi)

Two immaculate Finnish platoons of StuG 40 Ausf Gs seen on June 4, 1944, during Marshal Mannerheim's birthday parade at Enso, Finland. The Finns received 59 of what they called the "*Sturmi*" and they were numbered accordingly, as can be seen here. The "Ps." stands for *panssarivanaunu* (it means tank but was used for all Finnish AFVs); the 531 = *Sturmgeschütz*; and the final numbers identify the individual vehicles (1–59). This serial can often be found on the forward superstructure and/or on the driver's side of the rear hull. Note the 30 mm supplementary armor bolted onto the front, the loader's shield and MG, and the *fylfot* or hooked cross symbol. The Finns had been using the ancient swastika symbol (they call it the *hakaristi*) since 1918 before it was hijacked by the Nazis. The Finnish Air Force continued to use a version until 2020. The *Sturmis* carried an elongated version of the *hakaristi*—the *fylfot*—on their sides and often on the lower hull. The crews wear m/27 field caps and m/27 uniforms, and the leading commander has the two pips of a senior lieutenant. (SA-Kuva/Finnish Archives)

The next change involved the inclusion in some units of *Sturmhaubitzen*. On paper, this altered their order of battle to include 33 StuG III/IVs and 12 Sturmhaubitzen 42s. There were 3 x *Batterien* each of 2 x command StuG IIIs, 2 x *Züge* of four StuG IIIs, and 1 x *Zug* of four StuH 42s.

The *StuG-Brigaden* were usually held at corps or army level and assigned as the need arose. During 1944 many of the *StuG-Brigaden* became *Heeres-Sturmgeschütz-* or *Heeres-Sturmartillerie-Brigaden*. The difference between the two was an accompanying grenadier battery. The *Sturmgeschütz Begleit Batterien* (escort batteries) were introduced in early 1944 and KStN 448 of December 1, 1944, finally gave a specific outline of what they should comprise:

Batterieführer

- *Batterietrupp* (*Batterie* OC, medical officer, and various runners: total 10 men)
- 3 x *Züge* (each of CO, *Zugtrupp*, 3 x *Gruppen* each of 12 men: total 42 men x 3 = 126 men)
- *Pionierzug* (each of CO, *Zugtrupp*, 3 x *Gruppen* each of 14 men: total 51 men)
- *Batterietroß* (12 men, two trucks)

This gave a total of 198 officers and men. Those *StuG-Brigaden* that added a *Grenadier Batterie* were renamed *Heeres-Sturmartillerie-Brigaden*. Those that didn't remained *Heeres-Sturmgeschütz-Brigaden*.

As mentioned, the *StuG-Brigaden* were held at corps or army level. However, some units—such as Großdeutschland and Waffen-SS divisions—had their own *Brigaden*. StuGs were also to be found in independent *Batterien* (with necessary extra equipment) and, of course, were used as *Panzerjäger* in infantry units. These were initially *Kompanien*, but when the *Abteilungen* became *Brigaden*, so the PzJg-Kp became PzJg-Abt with the unit number changing by the addition of 1,000. StuGs also appeared in armored units, often in place of unavailable tanks.

***Sturmartillerie* Units**
Tessin identifies the following:

***Sturmartillerie-Abteilungen*:** 184, 185, 190–92, 197, 203, 204

***Sturmgeschütz-Abteilungen*:** 177, 184, 185, 189–92, 197, 200–3, 209, 210, 226, 228, 232, 236, 237, 239, 243–45, 249, 259, 261, 270, 276–81, 286, 300, 301, 303, 311, 322, 325, 341, 393, 394, 428, 600, 667, 902, 904, 905, 907–9, 911, 912, 914–16, 918, Burg, Großdeutschland

***Sturmgeschütz-Brigaden*:** 177, 184, 185, 189, 190, 191, 201–3, 209, 210, 226, 228, 232, 236, 237, 239, 243–45, 249, 259, 261, 270, 276–81, 286, 300, 301, 303, 311, 322, 325, 341, 393–98, 600, 667, 901, 902, 904, 905, 907, 909, 911, 912, 914, 920

***Heeres-Sturmartillerie-Brigaden*:** 184, 185, 202, 236, 239, 243, 249, 261, 277, 300, 303, 600, 667, 905, 911, 912, 1178

Other units: Sturmartillerie-Lehr-Brigade 111

Sturmgeschütz-Ersatz-Abteilungen: 200, 300, 400, 500, 600, 700

Sturmgeschützschule Burg Lehrabteilung

Sturmpanzer IV *Abteilungen*

There were four *Sturmpanzer-Abteilungen*—216, 217, 218, and 219. Each *Abteilung* was due 45 of the Sturmpanzer IV—with three in the *Stab* (an original allocation of three PzKpfw IIIs was changed to 3 x Sturmpanzer IV) and 14 in each of three *Kompanien* (4 in each of 3 *Züge* + 2 in *Kp Stab*).

Panzerjäger

At the start of the war all *Infanterie/Panzer/leichten/Gebirgs-Divisionen* had a *Panzer-Abwehr-Abteilung* composed of three 3.7 cm gun-equipped antitank companies and a 2 cm FlaK AA company. As the 3.7 cm proved increasingly ineffective, captured guns—particularly Belgian, Czech, and French 4.7 cm—were used. The *Panzer-Abwehr-Abteilungen* became *Panzerjäger-Abteilungen* from March 16, 1940.

Realizing their need for more mobile and heavier weapons, the first SP *Panzerjäger* was a Czech 4.7 cm gun on a PzKpfw I chassis. It saw service in France, the North African

An early StuG III L/24 of StuG-Abt 203 near the Dnieper and Smolensk in mid-1941. Note its markings on the superstructure side: the charging elephant indicates the *Abteilung*; the 33 identifies that it's the third vehicle in *Zug* (platoon) 3. (NARA)

desert, and on the Eastern Front. They were organized into *Abteilungen* of three *Kompanien*, each having nine vehicles—although these numbers were often not adhered to. In France the first *Abteilungen* were 521, 616, 643, and 670—only the former fighting throughout the campaign.

The success of the Panzerjäger I led to the development of antitank guns on Sfl from either Beute or obsolescent chassis. The follow-up to the Panzerjäger I was produced in 1941 on the Renault R35 chassis and equipped PzJg-Abt 559, 561, and 611. These *Abteilungen* were organized as a *Stab* and three *Kompanien* each of three *Züge* of three vehicles each. They took part in *Barbarossa* where the cold proved to be too much for the engines which froze. Nevertheless, repaired they continued to be used, particularly in occupation duties in the West.

The PzJg-Kp (mot S) establishment of February 1942 had two *Züge* each of three early Marder IIIs. By late 1942–early 1943 many of the *Panzerjäger* units in motorized and *Panzer-Divisionen* had SP elements in the form the later Marder III. The establishment of a PzJg-Kp (mot S) of June 1943 was two in the *Stab* and three *Züge* of four each—but very often the 14 became 10 with the *Stab* and each *Zug* losing a vehicle. There weren't sufficient vehicles to equip all *Infanterie-Divisionen* this way, although some received these vehicles. The establishment for a PzJg-Abt in November 1943 was the same as that of June; however, as time went on and German production geared up, the later *Infanterie-* and *Volksgrenadier Divisionen* of 1944 and 1945 had—on paper at least—an SP *Panzerjäger Kompanie* usually equipped with StuG IIIs and IVs or, latterly, the Jagdpanzer 38.

The *Gliederung* or structure of the *Division neuer Art* of October 1943 included 1 Kp with 14 heavy PaK (Sfl) 5 cm; 2 Kp with 10 *Sturmgeschütze*; and 3 Kp. with 9 FlaK 3.7 cm (mot). The nomenclature, as mentioned above, changed so that the StuG-Kp became StuG-Abt with a change to the number (addition of 1,000).

Production of what we know as the Hetzer stuttered until the middle of 1944 and never reached the 500 a month that were ordered. The first unit to receive its full complement of 45—three in the *Stab* and 14 in each of three *Kompanien*—was Heeres-Panzerjäger-Abteilung 731 in mid-July 1944. Other similar units followed: HPzJg-Abt 743, 741, 561, and 744. At the same time, the *Panzerjäger Kompanien* of the various infantry units were being reequipped with the new Jagdpanzer 38—but usually only 10 (*Stab*, plus three in each of three *Züge*) to equip as many units as possible.

It was used in the Type 1944 infantry or VGD divisions' *Panzerjäger* units. These usually comprised (on paper) a towed antitank gun company, a Flak company by this time upgunned from 2 cm to 3.7 cm, and an SP company that was usually made up of Sturmgeschütz IIIs or Jagdpanzer 38s.

The gendarme monitors the arrival of German troops in eastern Slovakia, 1944. This Kübelwagen has a tactical sign on the back identifying its parent unit—sPzJg-Abt 88; the symbol represents a self-propelled antitank gun. On the right rear there's also a unit insignia of a dagger and oak leaf used by sPzJg-Abt 88. (GF Collection)

Doyle & Jentz highlight the numbers at the start of *Unternehmen Wacht am Rhein*: 295 sent to the West to equip 18 *Panzerjäger-Kompanien* and HPzJg-Abt 741. Other units—such as 16. SS-PzGrenDiv—received Jagdpanzer 38s instead of the unavailable Jagdpanzer IV or PzKpfw IV/70. Jagdpanzer 38s also formed the principal component of the *Panzerjäger-Kompanien* of the *Panzerjagd-Brigaden* organized in January 1945.

The Jagdpanzer 38s proved mechanically reliable and on April 10, 1945, 489 were identified as operational on the Eastern Front (out of 661); 79 of 101 in the West; and 49 of 56 in Italy—pretty good for the end of the war.

The other workhorse of the *Panzerjäger* in the later was years was the Jagdpanzer IV which was mainly used in *Panzer-* and *Panzergrenadier-Divisionen*: the former two *Kompanien* of 10 each plus one in the *Stab*; the latter, 14 in each *Kompanie* and three in the *Stab* giving a total of 31 (on paper). While new units may have achieved these numbers, lack of vehicles meant actual numbers may have been different. In reality, these units were lucky to be able to field two platoons of StuG IIIs or obsolescent Marders brought back into service. This lack of the intended equipment is exemplified by the Jagdpanther *sPzJg-Abteilungen*, many of which sometimes had two Jagdpanzer IVs in three *Kompanien*. The PzKpfw IV/70 was a powerful weapon and often fulfilled the role of tanks and StuGs.

Schwere Panzerjäger-Abteilungen and _Panzerjäger-Abteilungen_ (Sfl)

Of great interest to enthusiasts, particularly modelers, these units often employed the largest and most potent of Germany's tracked tank destroyers: the Hornisse—renamed Nashorn in 1944 (for simplicity named Nashorn throughout this section); the Ferdinand, built on the 90 chassis of the Porsche's proposal for the Tiger (it too was renamed and became the Elefant in 1944); the Jagdpanther, the vehicle with probably the most potential as a *Panzerjäger*; and the enormous Jagdtiger that might have mounted the biggest gun but whose 72-tonne weight made it impractically heavy for its chassis. Used mainly on the Eastern Front—otherwise, only sPzJg-Abt 93 (Italy) and around 20 in the West with II./Pz-Regt 2—Nashorn *Abteilungen* were assigned to a larger unit, an *Armee* or *Korps*, and would then be sent out in small numbers as necessary. A Nashorn *Abteilung* would have a *Stab* (three vehicles) and three *Kompanien* of 14 Nashorn each—45 in total. The *Stab* would also have three SdKfz 7/1 for AA protection, and an SdKfz 251/8 ambulance halftrack. The Nashorn's main users were the *sPzJg-Abteilungen*:

Unit	Number	Dates in service
sPzJg-Abt 560	34	May 1943–Feb 1945
sPzJg-Abt 525	90	May 1943–Nov 1944
sPzJg-Abt 655	54	May 1943–Mar 1944
sPzJg-Abt 93	85	Jul 1943–Aug 1944
sPzJg-Abt 519	60	Sep 1943–Jun 1944
sPzJg-Abt 88	67	Dec 1943–Mar 1945
II./PzRegt 2	22	Nov–Dec 1944
sPzJg-Kp 669	17	Jan–Feb 1945

The organization of Ferdinand units was similar, each *Abteilung* receiving 45 vehicles: three in the *Abteilung Stab* which also had *Aufklärungs* and *Pioniere Züge*, and three SdKfz 7/1 for AA protection. Each *Kompanie*—there were three of them—had a *Stab* of two Ferdinands and four in each of three *Züge* (45 in total). For Kursk, the sPzJg-Abt 653 and 654 were combined with Sturmpanzer-Abteilung 216 (also 45 vehicles) in sPzJg-Regiment 656. Anderson quotes Guderian's report identifying "19 Ferdinand and 10 *Sturmpanzer* had to be completely written off: 40 Ferdinand and 17 *Sturmpanzer* were temporarily disabled, of which 20 and nine, respectively, could be repaired." The fighting there and elsewhere accounted for around half of the Ferdinands—only 50 returned to German for overhaul and modifications in October 1943—but they destroyed a lot of Soviet tanks and equipment. There's no doubt that the German crews showed more tactical astuteness, were often more experienced (because their vehicles were more survivable), and—most importantly—had better communication skills thanks to their radios and training. The Soviets, however, had had time to prepare their defenses (minefields), had substantial artillery and antitank defenses, and had the numbers. They had less need to repair than the Germans and could write off vehicles that the Germans would keep on their books (and not write off) for months.

While the exact cause of their losses is debated, the fact remains that the Ferdinands were susceptible to mine damage—40 were temporarily lost to mines until repaired—and were so heavy that retrieval was difficult and at times impossible. Lack of spare parts didn't help either. This was even though the *Abteilung* had a workshop, crane, and a *Bergegruppe* (recovery section) which was intended to utilize two SdKfz 20s or three SdKfz 9s. Either way, several of the vehicles lost perhaps could have been retrieved had they had heavier retrieval equipment.

The other two heavyweight *Panzerjäger* introduced in the later years of the war, the Jagdpanther and Jagdtiger, had similar organization, similar problems (delivery of vehicles, their weight, lack of spare parts, and reliability), and similar strengths (guns, armor, and—until mid-1944—training). A Jagdpanther *Abteilung* was, optimistically, due to receive 45 vehicles (three *Befehlswagen* in the *Stab*, with three *Kompanien* of 14). It also had a supply *Kompanie*, a workshop *Zug* (some with Bergepanthers), and a *Fliegerabwehrtrupp* (3 x SdKfz 7/1). However, this happened rarely and in September 1944 it was ordered that Jagdpanzer IV or *Sturmgeschütze* replace two of the *Kompanien*. An example of this was sPzJg-Abt 559—complete by the end of August 1944 with *Stab* and Jagdpanther *Kompanie* and two *Sturmgeschütz Kompanien*.

Only two *sPzJg-Abteilungen* received the Jagdtiger: 512 and 653—the latter being one of the original Nashorn units. The Jagdtigers were slow to arrive for 653: 12 in October 1944; more followed but some were still missing by the end of December. 512—Otto Carius's unit—fared even worse: its first vehicles only arrived at Sennelager on March 5, 1945. Cumbersome and unreliable, with insufficiently trained crews, most of the Jagdtigers were destroyed by their crews whilst immobile and unrecoverable.

Panzerartillerie

From the start the proponents of mobile warfare—particularly Lutz and Guderian—understood the need for SP guns. As early as 1934 *Panzer-Divisionen* were outlined with an artillery unit of three *Batterien* each of four guns. The trouble was that what they wanted—enough speed to keep with the tanks, short preparation for action, guns that could traverse 360°, and a

Men of 15. Infanterie-Division practice loading the 7.5 cm PaK 40 of a Marder I in southern France. The insignia on the right rear of the vehicle identifies the parent unit: 15. Infanterie. It represents the *Alte Römer Gebäude* (old Roman buildings) on the Römerberg in the old town of Frankfurt am Main. This is an unofficial insignia that harks back to a constituent element of the division, the Reichswehr's 81. Regiment. The tactical marking at left is the symbol for a motorized antitank unit—PzJg-Abt 15. The I above means 1. Kompanie (2. Kp had PaK 40s towed by Maultiers and 3. Kp had 2 cm FlaKs towed by trucks). (GF Collection)

dismountable gun—was extremely difficult to provide. It took time for their arguments to bear fruit, and by 1938 only a few "*Bunkerknacker*" (bunker busters) had been built incorporating SdKfz 8s and either 8.8 cm FlaK 18 or 10 cm K 18 guns. Panzer-Abwehr-Abt 8, with 10 of the former, fought in Poland. Organization was four *Kompanien*: one of 8.8 cm/SdKfz 8 combos in 1 Kp; two with towed 3.7 cm PaKs; and the last with towed 2 cm FlaK 30s. The concept proved its worth in speed, both over the ground and in readiness for deployment.

It was the Bison I that led to the first proper SPG unit, with six companies (each of six guns) formed in 1938 (sIG [Sfl] Kp 701–6) and issued to *Panzer-Divisionen*. How did they perform in France? In a word, badly. Anderson quotes a June 6, 1940, report to Oberbefehlshaber des Heeres that suggested that the gun was effective but the chassis on which it was mounted wasn't, partly because of their age and partly because they were too slow to keep up. Relegated to being used by the infantry, the weapon was easily damaged by AP ammunition through the thinly armored front gunshield.

However, the performance improved after that, mainly because of the extended training time following the fall of France. A report of September 18 said, "our crews have benefited from the long training phase and become accustomed to all mechanical vagaries and adept at correcting any faults." The bad news was that other areas that needed improvement couldn't be achieved by training: radio range and workshop amenities were both lacking. The units needed an SdKfz 7 and a flatbed trailer to improve retrieval.

Following the Bison I, another attempt to marry the sIG 33 with a suitable chassis led to 12 on the PzKpfw II in January and February 1942. These went to North Africa with sIG 33 Kp (mot S) 707 and 708. Unsuccessful mechanically, they were all lost by the end of 1943.

At the end of October 1942, the first of 24 sIG 33Bs—the sIG 33/1 mounted on a StuG III chassis—were delivered to StuG-Abt 177 and 244 in Stalingrad. Designed to be used in urban areas, in total 12 reached the city before it was surrounded. The other 12 took their place in Sturm-Infanterie-Geschütz-Batterie/Lehr-Bataillon (Assault Infantry Gun Batterie/Demonstration Battalion) XVII which was badly mauled trying to relieve 6. Armee. The remainder became part of 9./Regiment 201 and some were still active in late 1944. One of these can be seen in the Kubinka Tank Museum.

This 15 cm sIG 33 Sfl auf PzKpfw I Ausf B (also known as the Sturmpanzer I) is seen at a firing position in the suburbs of Moscow, November 1941. One of six independent companies set up to provide the *Panzer-Divisionen* with artillery support, sIG Kompanie 704 was assigned to 5. Panzer-Division in April 1940. This photograph shows well the height of the vehicle, the open firing platform, and its markings: the yellow "X" denoting 5. Panzer, 704 for its company, and the C on the side identifying it as the third gun in the unit. The Sturmpanzer I was an uncomfortable vehicle, and some of the crew traveled in halftracks with the guns. (albumwar2.com)

In 1941 and 1942 a range of captured vehicles were converted to carry such guns as the 7.5 cm PaK 40, 10 cm leFH 18, 10 cm leFH 16, and 15 cm sFH 13/1. Most of these vehicles were French, although the British Vickers Light Tank Mk VI was also used. These conversions were handled by the remarkable Alfred Becker and his team linked with Alkett. Perhaps their best-known handiwork are those mounted on the Lorraine 37L Schlepper and the Hotchkiss H39. Becker went on to provide 21. Panzer-Division with a range of vehicles used to good effect in Normandy in 1944.

In 1943 the sIG 33 was put onto the PzKpfw 38(t) chassis to produce the Grille. From 1943 these were to be supplied to *Panzer-* and *Panzergrenadier-Divisionen*. In the latter a PzGr-Regt (gep) would have a 10. schwere Geschütz Kompanie with a couple of SdKfz 250s with the *Stab* and three *Züge* each of a halftrack and two Grillen.

The next significant SP guns were the light 10.5 cm leFH 18/2 auf Gw II Wespe, which was produced on the PzKpfw II chassis in 1943–44, and the heavy 15 cm sFH 18/1 auf Gw IV Hummel. Production of the former was canceled because "it did not prove satisfactory" (Anderson); production of the latter continued until the plant was bombed heavily in March 1945.

Both entered service at the end of May 1943 and equipped several units at Kursk. The Wespes could be found with 17. Panzer-Division (12), 3. PzGr-Div (18), 29. PzGr-Div (18), PzGr-Div Großdeutschland (12), 1. SS-Panzer-Division LSSAH (12), and 2. SS-Panzer-Division Das Reich (12). In total there were 60 Hummels at Kursk with the Panzer-Divisionen 1., 2., 4., 6.–17., 20., and 24.–26.; 90. PzGr, PzGr-Div Großdeutschland, 18. Art-Div, and 1.–3. SS-PzDiv. By the end of 1943, Wespes could be found in 31 *Panzer-* or *Panzergrenadier-Divisionen*, six in each of the two light batteries of their *Artillerie-Regimenter*; many also were equipped with its weaponless *Munitionsträger* variant. Successful in the Soviet Union, less so in Italy because of the stress put on the chassis by the mountainous terrain, the Wespe had been seen as a stop gap, but no other light SP followed it. There were still over 300 in service in March 1945, and it had seen use by most of the army and *SS-Pz-* or *PzGr-Divisionen*.

The Hummel was similarly widespread, by end of 1943 equipping 37 units—six each in a *Batterie* in mainly army and *SS-Panzer-* or *Panzergrenadier-Divisionen* but also 14 each in several *Artillerie-Regimenter* or *-Abteilungen*. It also suffered from the terrain in Italy but acquitted itself well elsewhere. The weight of its ammunition reduced the amount that could be carried aboard and necessitated an unarmed *Munitionsträger* variant.

| Mobility

It seems obvious to say it, but the raison d'être of AFVs is to add mobility to land forces: to allow them to carry into battle heavy weapons and support vehicles that would otherwise not be available to foot soldiers. The German Army used large numbers of horses to drag their heavy equipment around but that could never match the speed of the *Panzers* and that's why they turned to other tracked vehicles to ensure that *Panzerjager*, SP guns, and infantry in halftracks could keep pace.

The problem with that mobility is that it comes with a price. There needs to be dedicated teams of people to ensure the AFVs are roadworthy, to retrieve them when they break down, and mend them. They also must deal with problems involving sophisticated machinery—radios, gunsights, heavy weapons—all the time having to cope with conditions in the field rather than back at home near the factories that built the vehicles, close to amenities, supplies, and more technicians.

And, as any report of AFV availability shows, the *Panzerwärte*—AFV mechanics—were needed all the time. As examples, 2./ and 3./StuG-Abt 202 reported in early March 1943 that they had 12 StuGs. Adding the one the *Stab* had, that gave them 13 in total, but only 75 percent of these—nine—were combat ready. It was the engines that were the main problem. One of the reasons for this was lack of a maintenance service and towing section.

Mobile cranes for maintenance units were gear-driven, operated by manual cranks, either wheeled or tracked. This crane is a Bilstein-Drehkran 3-tonne lift swing crane on a Büssig-Nag 500A heavy truck, that had been modified by Bilstein. Here it's being used in the Soviet Union in August 1943 to remove or replace the 7.5 cm StuK 40 L/43 on a StuG III Ausf F chassis. (Bundesarchiv, Bild 101I-154-1991-24A/Dreyer/CC-BY-SA 3.0)

Supply depots are as important a part of military life as weapons. The white cross on these jerrycans indicates water—always a precious commodity. Note the snow-chains on the truck wheels. An April 1943 photo. (GF Collection)

Refueling a StuG 40 Ausf G. Fuel was originally gasoline but predominantly, as the war continued, synthetic; by 1944 Germany's synthetic fuel plants were producing 124,000 barrels a day. Here, in the Finnish forest, fuel is hand-pumped from 200-liter *Kraftstoff Fässer* (fuel drums), in this case from the back of a vehicle. Each drum had two raised rolling rings, just visible in the photo behind the pumper's lower leg and would be stamped for the arm they belonged to. For smaller quantities there was the 20-liter *Wehrmacht-Einheitskanister*—or jerrycan as we know it, a name coined by the British out of respect for a fuel container far superior to theirs. These were filled at a depot, a bowser, or directly from the larger drums and transported to a location to be poured directly into a fuel tank. One is seen by the boot on the left in the photo. The StuG III held between 300–20 liters (79–85 US gal), giving a range of about 155 km (96 mi) but considerably less when offroad. (SA-kuva/Finnish Archives)

Crossing bridges must be carefully handled, minimum speed 5 mph, keep to the middle of the bridge, 35 yds vehicle spacing, and the commander of the assault guns must cooperate with the officer in charge of the bridge. Unfortunately, the local bridging in the Soviet Union wasn't always as strong as expected. The towing cables at the rear are in readiness for an attempt to retrieve the vehicle: no easy task at 20 tonnes and that angle. With no specialist tracked heavy recovery vehicles at this stage of the war, recovery would more likely be attempted by several linked tracked or half-tracked vehicles such as the 18t SdKfz 9. Note the charging elephant symbol of StuG-Abt 203 on rear and turret side and the two-digit turret number 33. This is a typical early *Barbarossa* numbering method (later increasing to three) where 3 = *Zug* and the second 3 = vehicle. (NARA)

This bridge has seen some engineer work: a StuG III Ausf B crosses a makeshift wooden bridge at the front near Novgorod. The groups either side look to be a mixture of Germans (shoulder straps and collars) and Hiwis (Soviets used as helpers) in their distinctive pullover blouses. With the Luftwaffe dominating the skies recognition panels were essential to prevent what we'd call "blue on blue" events today. The prepared timber in the background is being readied to build a more substantial bridge. (NAC)

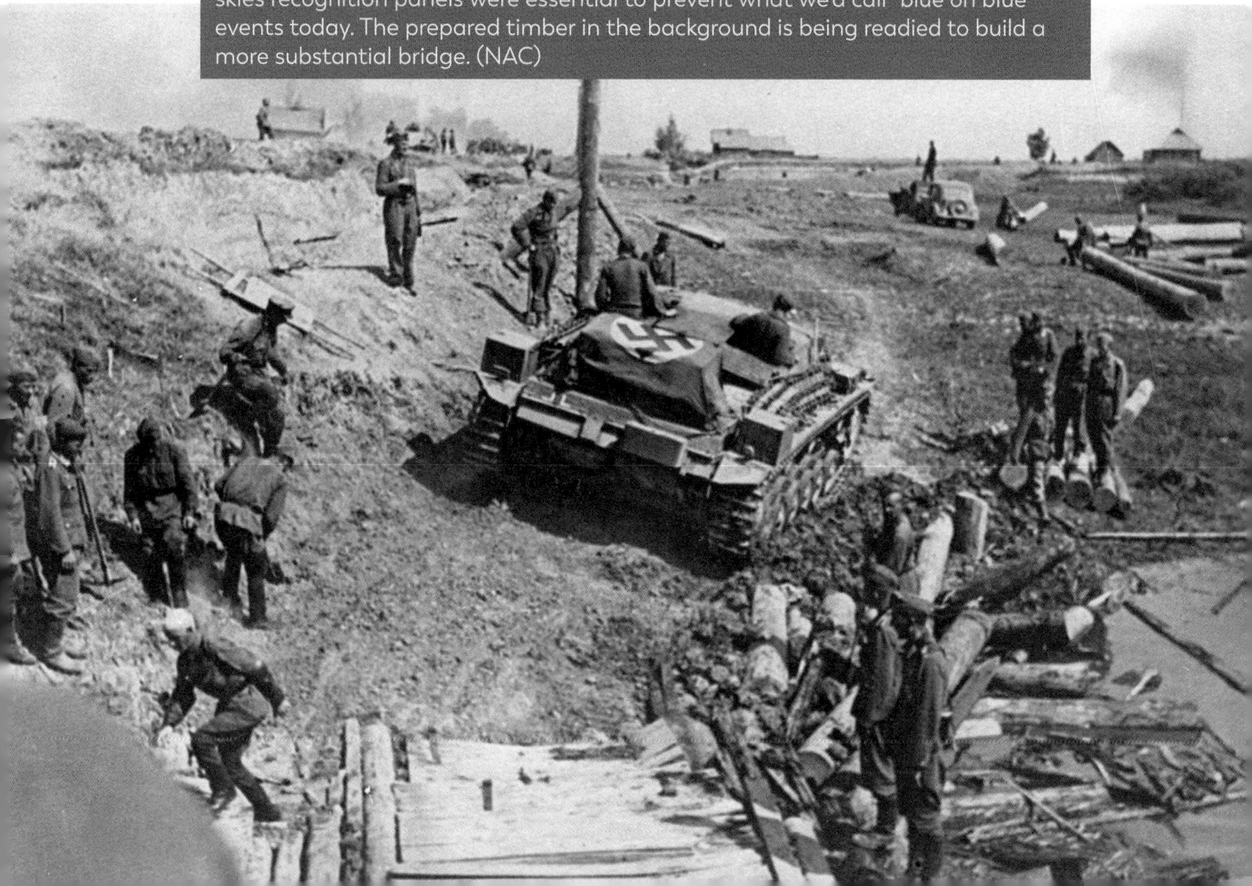

Trains were hugely important for moving men, munitions, and armor. The StuG III weighed around 23 tonnes and could be carried on a Typ Ommr two-axle flatbed, minus the usual stake stanchions that were made of metal or wood. The Typ Ommr was built 1939–41. The *Kriegsbauart* (wartime class) railway wagons were developed during the war. One category of the new builds was for tank transport: eight- or 12-wheel heavy flat cars. Additional wheels were essential as tanks got heavier and heavier—the Panther weighed 46 tonnes and the Tiger 57 tonnes so the need was obvious. Note the wooden wheel blocks front and rear to prevent rolling, the tensioned hawsers, and the stanchion slots along the side. (Marics Zoltán/Fortepan/Hungarian Archives)

On March 14, nine of the 13 were operational, on the 20th eight, on the 27th nine again. On the Western Front the story was the same. Stephen Zaloga in New Vanguard 298 said of the Jagdpanthers of sPzJg-Abt 654: "on July 18, 1944, a day after the battalion entered combat, of 25 vehicles on hand only eight were operational." He goes on to note that on August 1, 16 of 26 were in repair and on August 12 only two of the 21 Jagdpanthers left were operational, with 19 in repair.

All this meant the engineers and mechanics who kept the *Panzer*, *Sturmgeschütz*, *Panzerjäger*, or SP artillery units on the road needed to be well trained, competent, and brave. Each unit had its own mechanics, but the first people in the chain were the crews who had the initial responsibility for maintenance. Every time a tank stopped for any length of time there were things to be checked and tightened, greased, and lubricated.

Repairs that were necessary were almost always dealt with at the front—usually at workshops which could deal with as many as 30–40 tanks whose repairs might take as long as two weeks, depending on how long it took to get

One of the *Instandsetzungsstaffel*'s most important assets was the SdAh 116 22t low loader trailer for AFVs, seen here carrying a StuG Ausf A. (World War photos)

spare parts if they couldn't be cannibalized from more badly damaged vehicles. Less than 10 percent of damaged vehicles went back to the manufacturers for repair.

Much of the combat damage tended to be from antitank rifles and mines. Damage to tracks and the occasional road wheel could often be catered for by the crew themselves using the jack each tank carried. Problems with drive wheels or return rollers could require more attention and usually a tow back to a repair shop—the SdKfz 7s or 9s were the main prime movers—but as vehicles got heavier, a more specialist vehicle was required (it took three SdKfz 7s to pull a Tiger). *Bergepanzer* recovery vehicles were few and far between. The result was that too many of the expensive "big cats" had to be destroyed because of minor automotive problems or even running out of fuel.

The maintenance sections of *StuG Batterien* the *Instandsetzungsstaffel* or *Gruppen*—combined a range of skills as outlined in the various KStNs (from www.wwiidaybyday.com). Below are example outlines of several units' personnel:

StuG-Batterie Instandsetzungsstaffel (*KStN 446 of November 1, 1941*)
7 x StuGs (1 x *Stab*; 2 each x 3 *Züge*)
Manpower: commander, motor sergeant, weapons NCO, 1 motorcycle rider (motor sergeant in sidecar), 6 x *Panzerwärte* mechanics (2 also co-drivers, 1 welder, 1 electrician, 2 x engine fitters), armorer's assistant, 7 drivers, and 2 engine fitters
Vehicles: 1 x *kleiner Instandsetzungskraftwagen*—small maintenance motor vehicle with a built-in toolbox—(Kfz 2/40), 3 x trucks (one general, two for workshop equipment and spare parts), 1 SdKfz 9 18-tonne heavy tractor unit, 1 x 22-tonne low loader trailer for AFVs (SdAh 116)

StuG-Abteilung Instandsetzungsstaffel (*KStN 446B of November 1, 1942*)
10 x StuGs (1 x *Stab*; 3 each x 3 *Züge*)
Same as KStN 446 except:
Manpower: Extra 2 x *Panzerwärte* mechanics; 1 x low-loader handler
Vehicles: change from 2 x trucks for workshop equipment and spare parts to 3 x trucks, 2 spare parts and 1 for workshop equipment

StuG-Brigade Instandsetzungsdienste for batteries of 10/14 StuGs (*KStN 416 of June 1, 1944*)
10 x StuGs (1 x *Stab*; 3 each x 3 *Züge*) or 14 x StuGs (2 x *Stab*; 4 each x 3 *Züge*)
1) *Waffen und Gerät-Instandsetzungsstaffel* (Weapons and equipment maintenance section)
Manpower: armorer, weapons NCO, radio NCO, leading signals mechanic, signals mechanic, armored vehicle radio mechanic, 2 x armorer's assistants, driver
Vehicles: 1 x 2-tonne truck, 1 x 4.5-tonne truck as armorer's workshop

2) *Leichter Kfz-Instandsetzungszug* (Light vehicle maintenance section)
Manpower: motor workshop transport repair shop foreman, leading craftsman, engine fitter sergeant, 4 x senior craftsmen (1 engine fitter, 2 gearbox fitters, 1 fitter), 8 x engine fitters (2 co-drivers as well), 5 x gearbox fitters (2 co-drivers as well), 2 x electricians, 1 x plumber, 1 x turner, 6 x drivers, cook
Vehicles: 1 x light cross-country passenger car (probably a VW Typ 82); 1 x 2-tonne truck for small field kitchen, 3 x trucks, 1 x SdAh 24 to carry heavy machine set A, arc-welding unit on a trailer, with accessories, Kfz 100 *Bilstein* swing crane motor vehicle (lifting force 3 tonnes)

Early spring of 1943, from the album of Leutnant W. Böhm, who transferred from StuG-Abt 190 to StuG-Abt 189. This StuG 40 Ausf G has extra bolted-on 30 mm frontal armor, *Winterketten*, and an interesting custom-made mantlet cover. Note the tactical symbol on the front plate (it signifies an assault gun). Each StuG man wears the General Assault Badge and the one on the right a black wound badge and an EK II ribbon. (Akira Takiguchi)

3) *Ersatzteilgruppe* (Spare parts group)
Manpower: motor sergeant, spare parts manager, 6 men (incl. 4 drivers)
Vehicles: 4 x 4.5-tonne trucks for spare parts

4) *Bergetrupp* (Recovery Troop)
Manpower: 4 x mechanics (1 SdAh 116 handler, 3 also co-drivers)
Vehicles: 3 x SdKfz9 18-tonne prime movers, 1 x SdAh 116 22-tonne flatbed trailer for AFVs

Winter

All AFV crews found the snow and wintry conditions hard going. First, the extreme cold led to innumerable problems as lubricants froze. When the crew did get the vehicles moving, snow and ice wedged into tracks and wheels. The experience of the winter of 1941/42 shocked the OKW and led to changes, including the official instruction of August 1942 *Kraftfahrzeuge im Winter—Anweisungen für Wartung und Bedienung* (Motor vehicles in winter—Instructions for maintenance and operation). It was issued by the OKH, notably the Army Weapons Office, Development and Testing Division, and issued a range of instructions from putting antifreeze in radiators to warming the engines of new equipment as it reached the front and ensuring that the correct fuel and lubricants were used.

One important area was keeping fighting compartments warm. To do this, radiator hot air was fed in through a pipe (for example, in the Hummel). The problem with this was carbon monoxide and gunners and commanders were strictly ordered to watch the indicators and test paper to ensure the crew wasn't asphyxiated through leaking exhaust fumes. There were also special winter fans to be installed. Engine coolant was kept from icing up thanks to the Panzer-Kühlwasserheizgerät 42 that was a pump to extract the water, blowtorch heaters to warm it, and another pump to replace it in the vehicle. Weapons had to carefully handled; optical equipment had to be protected from fogging and icing up—usually by being rubbed with Glasil.

There were also many different ice cleats and special tracks—although these were less necessary for vehicles with wider tracks (such as the Jagdpanther and Jagdtiger). Because they used the same tracks, the Sturmgeschütze III and IV were able to use the same as those for the PzKpfw III and IV: the *Hammerstollen, Mittelstollen* (where *stollen* = cleat), and *Schneegreifer* (snow grippers). They were better than nothing but took a long time to affix

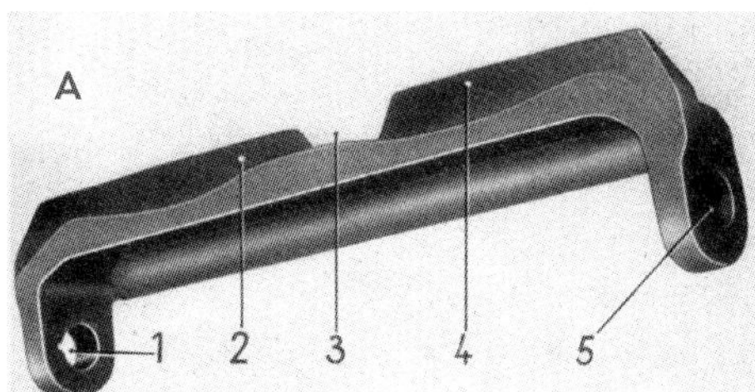

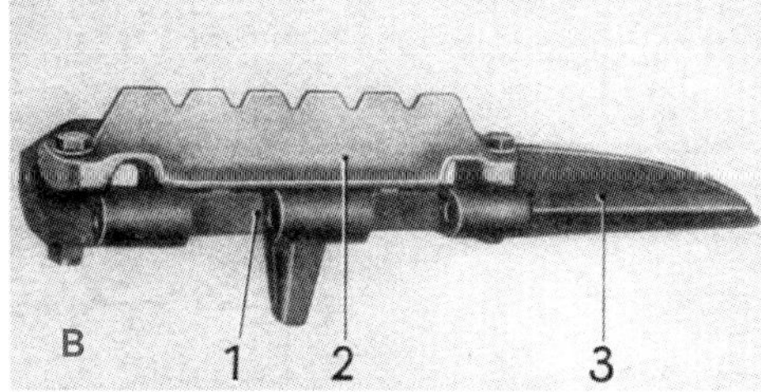

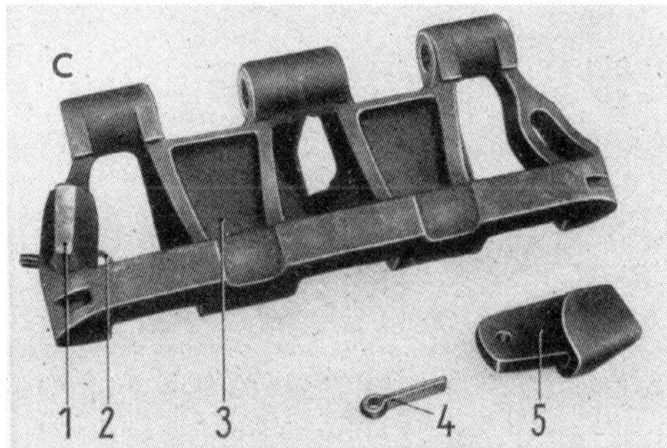

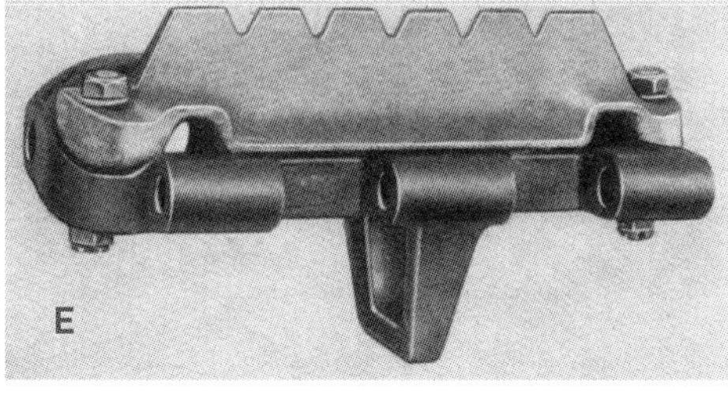

Cleats and Grippers

A One-piece gripper for PzKpfw 38(t):
1. Hole for track pin; 2. Left running surface of the grip; 3. Center cutout; 4. Right running surface of the grip; 5. Hole for track pin.

B Link in a length of snow tracks used with PzKpfw III and IV:
1. Track link; 2. Snow gripper; 3. Widening of the track link.

C Hammer cleat set in track (view from above) as used by PzKpfw IIIs and IVs:
1. Hammer cleat; 2. Split pin; 3. Caterpillar track; 4. Split pin; 5. Hammer cleat.

D Center cleat for PzKpfw III and IV:
1. Cleat, from below; 2. Spring catch;
3. Cleat, from above; 4 Hard nose.

E Snow gripper used for PzKpfw IIIs and IVs.

(From Directives on Machine Maintenance under Weather Conditions of 27 August 1942 via Wikipedia Commons)

and all too often broke or became detached. *Winterketten* (winter tracks), that extended outwards to give a greater track width and, therefore, more floatation, were developed in 1942. The *Winterketten* weren't a particular success. There were problems with track breakages and transmissions, and they tended to snap when they encountered something solid. They also couldn't be used with *Schürzen*.

In 1944, *Ostketten* (literally, East tracks) were developed to try and deal with the impassable muddy conditions of the *rasputitsa*—the period in fall and spring when rain and snow/ice thaw turned the roads of Eastern Europe into rivers of mud. The *Ostketten* were less likely to snap, could be used with *Schürzen*, and proved better than the *Winterketten* in mud as they accumulated less detritus.

Tactics

To begin with, the StuG wasn't to be used in an antitank role and would only engage enemy tanks in self-defense. That all changed when the *Langrohren* came in and made clear what had been apparent even with the short 7.5 cm L/24: the StuGs were ideal *Panzerjäger*. The U.S. Army's *Tactical and Technical Trends* (Vol. I, No. 11: July 1943) put this down to a combination of the longer gun and the arrival of hollow-charge ammunition, which achieved good armor-piercing performance at relatively low muzzle velocities. The article quoted Red Army sources:

> The Germans make extensive use of self-propelled guns as assault artillery. Their most important mission is to destroy the opposition's antitank and heavy infantry weapons. ...
>
> Assault batteries, which are assigned a limited number of targets, have the mission of supporting the attacks of the infantry, and of destroying the opposition's heavy infantry weapons and strong points disclosed during the attack. In supporting tank attacks, the self-propelled artillery assumes some of the normal tasks of the heavier tanks, including the destruction of antitank guns.

The *Sturmgeschütz* was always at risk from enemy infantry. It had poor all-round vision and no turret. Early in 1944 the German Army came up with a way of providing organic infantry support to the *Sturmgeschütz-Brigaden* and *-Abteilungen*: the *Begleit Batterie*. It had three escort platoons—one for every 10 assault guns. On the march, the grenadiers sat on the vehicles. Once in range of the enemy, they got off and provided close protection. However, Guderian was at pains to stress that self-defense wasn't just a matter for the escorting grenadiers: "Each part of the battery must always be prepared to defend itself against attacks by enemy infantrymen and to have to fight with naked weapons. ... If the assault gun is in close combat, it is almost always most advantageous to conduct the fight from the gun. Getting out gives the enemy the opportunity to shoot the crew. ... Only if an assault gun has become immobilized and its destruction by enemy action is imminent may the crew leave it. The gun must be destroyed by explosives. Important parts such as self-propelled gun telescopic sights, radio equipment and radio documents must not fall into enemy hands." (NAC)

Panzerjäger I of Panzerjäger-Abteilung 605 in North Africa. There are reports of three destroyed Matilda tanks at 400 m range in one action by using the rare tungsten rounds. (NARA)

The assault artillery never serves as antitank artillery in an attack; only in self-defense does it open fire at short range, shooting armor-piercing shells against tanks. Its shell has almost no effect against heavy tanks.

The battery is part of the combat echelon, and marches ahead of the trains. All seven guns and three armored supply vehicles are in this echelon. In deploying for battle the guns come first, moving abreast toward the front and ready for instant action. The guns of the platoon commanders are on the flanks. The battery commander is stationed to the rear, in a position which is dictated by the type of firing and the terrain. Behind him, the supply vehicles move by bounds from one protected position to another.

If a position lacks cover, these vehicles follow at a considerable distance, maintaining radio communication with the rest of the battery.

In carrying out its special task of facilitating an infantry breakthrough into the rear of the opposition's defenses, the assault battery may follow one of two methods of maneuver: it may take part in the initial assault, or it may be held in reserve and not committed until the hostile dispositions have been discovered. In all instances the battery cooperates closely with the supported infantry battalion or company.

Assault guns use direct fire. To achieve surprise, they move forward stealthily. In supporting an infantry attack under heavy enemy fire, assault guns halt briefly to fire on targets, which offer the greatest danger to the infantry. The assault guns fire a few times and then disappear to take part in the battle from other positions. When an assault artillery battalion is attached to an infantry division cooperating with Panzer units in an attack, the battalion's primary mission is to destroy the hostile antitank defenses. If the battalion is supporting tanks in a breakthrough, its batteries seek positions permitting good observation. In other cases, each battery moves into the attack after the first wave of tanks, and as soon as the latter encounters opposition, the assault guns cover them with protecting fire. It is believed that the Germans regard close cooperation between the assault battery and the first echelon of tanks as essential in effecting a quick destruction of antitank defenses.

If hostile tanks counterattack, the German antitank guns engage them, and the assault artillery unit seeks to destroy the hostile guns which are supporting the attacking tanks. When the German antitank artillery is unable to stop the hostile tanks, as a last resort, the self-propelled assault guns engage the tanks, opening fire on them with armor-piercing shells at 650 yards or less.

In the pursuit, the assault guns give the infantry close support to strengthen the latter's fire power.

The most important role of the assault battery in defense appears to be in support of counterattacks. However, in special instances, they have been used as artillery to reinforce the division artillery. When an assault battery is to support a counterattack, it is freed from all other tasks. The battery, knowing the limits within

Wolfgang Willrich's portrayal of Hugo Primozic (1914–96). Willrich had been commissioned to draw all *Ritterkreuzträger* and Primozic was the first NCO in the history of the German Army to be awarded the *Ritterkreuz* and, later, the *Eichenlaub* (Oak Leaves). With the rank of *Wachtmeister*, he was a platoon leader in 2./StuG-Abt 667 which was sent to the Rzhev Salient. On September 15, 1942, Primozic is said to have destroyed 24 Soviet tanks. For this action he was awarded the Knight's Cross of the Iron Cross. On November 24, during another Soviet assault he claimed another seven. By December his tally was 60. In January 1943, in recognition of his achievements he was awarded the Oak Leaves to his *Ritterkreuz* and his entire crew were awarded the German Cross in Gold. Promoted to *Leutnant*, he was assigned to a training unit for the remainder of the war. (RCT)

> which the counterattack will operate, acts just as it would in supporting an infantry attack. Assault-battery officers and infantry commanders jointly make a careful reconnaissance of the area in which the counterattack is to take place.
>
> The most vulnerable points of a German self-propelled assault gun, according to the Russians, are the moving parts, the rear half of the fighting compartment, the observation apparatus, and the aiming devices.

A later report in *Intelligence Bulletin* of December 1944 reasserts much of what was said in 1942:

> In the attack, assault guns move in batteries, in extended order, with distances between vehicles varying according to visibility. They rely entirely on the infantry for protection and try to stay near the infantry for whom they are furnishing support. Single guns operate under the orders of the nearest infantry commander, but the Germans stress the fact that batteries must be kept intact. … Assault guns fire from concealed positions, whenever possible. They are not dug in but may seek cover either beside or inside masonry walls, as illustrated above. An assault gun in the hotel in Cassino was most effective in supporting the "Green Devils" of the German 1st Parachute Division, who were defending the town.
>
> In pursuit, most assault guns move with the advance guard of the advance detachment. Here they will be sited to deal with any weak resistance delaying the advance, and to combat tanks. However, assault guns are not regarded as reconnaissance vehicles. The Germans forbid their use as armored cars, or as accompanying support for patrols of whatever type. They are a shock weapon.
>
> In the face of moderate resistance, infantry with light machine guns may ride on assault guns. These infantrymen dismount when fired on and proceed to protect

the gun from infantry attack. Assault guns unprotected by infantry are extremely vulnerable.

Assault guns form the backbone of units assigned to seize and defend commanding terrain features. Slit trenches are dug for the protection of personnel. The assault guns are never dug in but remain ready to make the most of their characteristic mobility.

When withdrawal becomes necessary, assault guns are allotted to the commander of the rear guard. They normally travel with the rearmost troops, but since they have only one exterior-mounted light machine gun, they continue to rely on infantry protection.

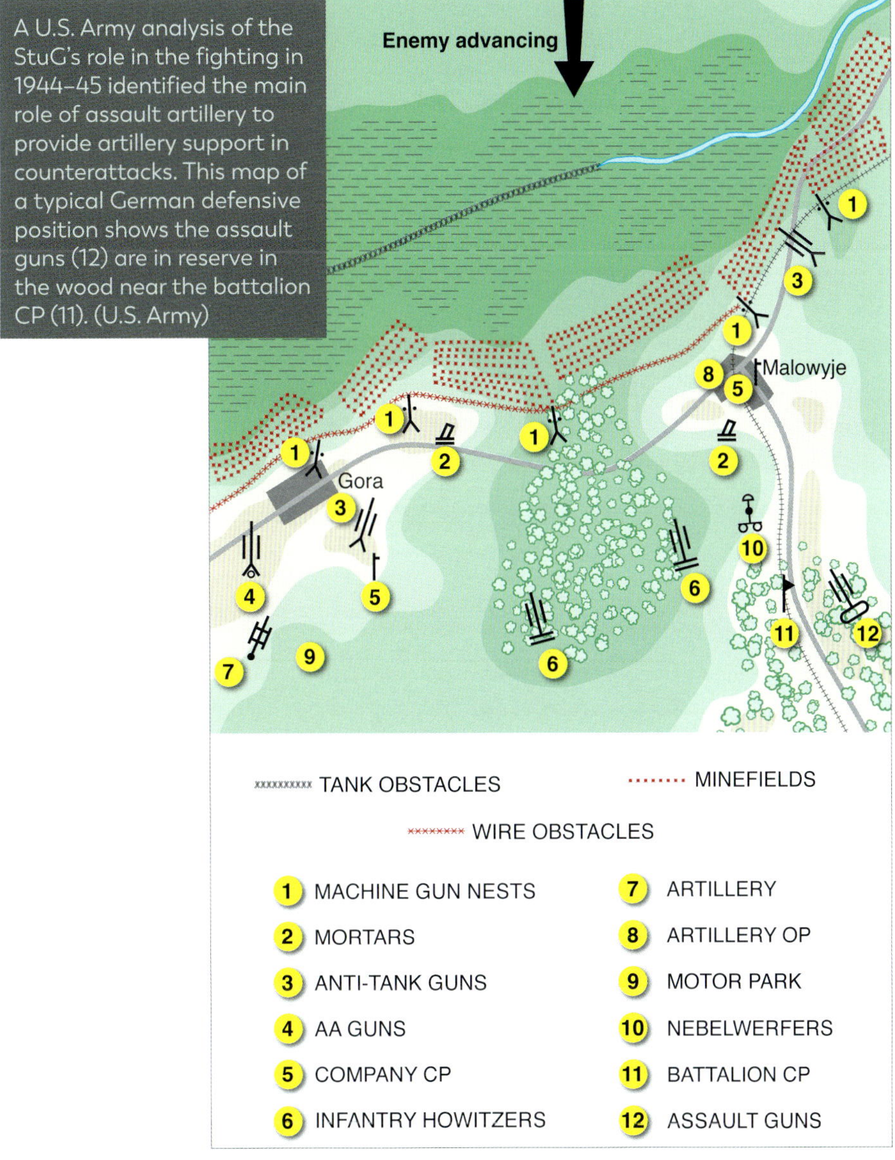

A U.S. Army analysis of the StuG's role in the fighting in 1944–45 identified the main role of assault artillery to provide artillery support in counterattacks. This map of a typical German defensive position shows the assault guns (12) are in reserve in the wood near the battalion CP (11). (U.S. Army)

In the withdrawal, the task of assault guns is to hold off enemy infantry until German infantry has disengaged. Sections leapfrog back, covering each other. Orders for withdrawal are given over the radio by the liaison officer with the rear-guard commander.

In attacks on fortified towns and villages, assault guns advance by batteries. Their mission is to destroy the foremost houses. After the infantry has broken into the edge of the town or village, the guns of a battery split up, and, by previous arrangement, join the various infantry–engineer assault groups and fight with them.

In village and street fighting, assault guns are considered most useful in breaking up roadblocks, barricades, and fortified houses. Here an assault gun advances, after knocking out a gun defending a barricade of paving stones. Assault guns are also used to provide direct fire against the embrasures, and other vulnerable points, of fortified positions. In missions of this type, they work with infantry–engineer teams seeking to break into the hostile position. Assault guns were first used for this purpose in France.

In case of a major German breakthrough, assault guns are often withdrawn once open country has been reached and the danger of counterattack has passed. They regroup en masse, while the job of pursuing the enemy and exploiting the breakthrough is taken over by tanks belonging to armored divisions. When tanks encounter difficult infantry-defended terrain or fortified positions, the assault guns are again brought forward into combat.

Tactics of *Panzerjäger* Units

The monthly *Nachrichtenblatt der Panzertruppen* provided *Panzer*, *Panzerjäger*, and *Sturmgeschütz* troops with information, propaganda, and lessons to be learnt. It looked at new equipment and how it should be handled, using reports from the battlefield to instruct its readers. The following article looks at the use of the Jagdpanzer IV. It starts by saying how well the vehicle had performed, and how its armor had proved resilient against fire from 7.62 cm antitank guns, antitank rifles, with no losses due to enemy action. (It's interesting to note that "no losses" doesn't mean that the unit didn't lose any vehicles. It simply means that they were all recovered by the *I-Dienste*, the maintenance services.) It starts, however, with the well-worn theme of fragmented deployment and how subordination to units smaller than the regiment leads to sections of the Jagdpanzer IV regiment being parceled out to be used in small numbers. This leads, the report emphasizes, to "unnecessary losses. It is therefore necessary for the commander of a Jagdpanzer IV unit to enforce the unit's unified deployment through clear proposals and not to give up control of the command." It goes on:

> 2. The order was given by higher authorities to also take non-operational tank destroyers into battle and to install immobilized tank destroyers as stationary antitank guns. The implementation of this order was bound to lead to the loss of these tank destroyers. For this reason, the commander of a Jagdpanzer IV unit must make it clear with all his might that the use of an immobile tank destroyer is pointless, since it cannot turn with the chassis without a running engine and—deprived of its mobility—is a bare target for the enemy or must be blown up. It must also be pointed out that most technical damage can be repaired in a matter of hours

A battery of Sturmpanzer I Bison 15 cm sIG 33 SP guns of Kompanie 705 of 7. Panzer-Division prepares for action. Assault artillery's chief mission is to support infantry in the attack by virtue of its armor, maneuverability, cross-country abilities, and rapidity in firing. Well spaced when on the move, it must be used in leapfrog fashion when operating with an infantry division. In exceptional circumstances a battery may accompany each combat team, normally kept at intervals between the advance and main body and under command of the column commander. (NARA)

or a few days, so that the tank destroyer in question is then fully operational and available to the troops again, whereas if such orders are carried out it will be lost. A responsible unit leader must therefore use all means possible to free up tanks that are not ready for use so that they can be rebuilt.

3. The use of Jagdpanzer IVs in unclear terrain without supervision by grenadiers often leads to the loss of the tank due to the approach of enemy tank destroyers. The permanent subordination of a grenadier unit to a tank destroyer (assault gun) detachment has proven to be extremely successful. The reinforced grenadier company subordinated to the detachment had already fully adapted to its fighting style of accompanying and supervising tank destroyers against tank destroyers after the first battle. It was also able to carry out independent attacks and counterattacks with a limited target under the fire cover of the tank destroyers and to fight down enemy heavy tanks that were identified by assault troop operations, and which could not be caught by the tank destroyers' weapons.

4. Attacking infantry targets with HE shells, which is required of the grenadiers only because of its morale effect, is not compatible with the limited ammunition available. The bow machine gun performs excellently at all target distances if the commander provides strict fire control. The use of HE shells must be limited to identified heavy weapons against closed units and to self-defense. For self-defense, reserves of all types of ammunition must be secured in an unassailable manner. It is proposed that for the Jagdpanzer IV, the grenades be placed in the holders to the left of the commander and that one box of belted machine-gun ammunition be stored on each of these. Ammunition for pistols and submachine guns and five egg grenades should be carried by the crew.

5. The use of Jagdpanzer units without sufficient maintenance services and towing equipment leads to unnecessary losses of tanks. The independent use of such units or individual tanks is therefore to be rejected as long as technical support by the *Instandsetzungsdienste* or similar units is not regulated.

6. In unclear situations that arose during the fighting for Baranowicze and the subsequent deployments, damaged tanks from other units were pushed along the roads used for supply and, because they were too slow, were reached and blown up by the enemy. In this case, it turned out to be useful to deploy I-Dienste near railway lines and tow damaged tanks there under the leadership of an energetic and

prudent officer (made mobile with wheeled vehicles) so that they could be loaded in the event of an enemy threat. In this way, when the enemy damaged tanks, the division recovered 17 Jagdpanzer IVs, three PzKpfw IVs, and a Hungarian tank by loading them onto railway routes far outside its sector.

7. Through appropriate training and under the supervision of an energetic officer, it was possible in all cases to remove the equipment from the Jagdpanzer IV that was prepared for demolition, even under strong enemy pressure, and to recover it by the crews, in some cases despite being surrounded by the enemy. The equipment was carried by the crews of two Jagdpanzer IVs through the enemy at night. Removal of the equipment, including radios and converters, as well as preparation for detonation and its implementation must be taught as part of the training.

8. Medical care for the seriously wounded in mobile combat has proven to be particularly difficult at night. The detachment had no ambulances or medical armored personnel carriers. The following is therefore suggested: during night-time combat, a hollow about a meter deep is dug under the commander's tank, lined with blankets and tarpaulins and covered on the sides with blankets to protect against light. In this hollow, the medical officer can treat the wounded in full light and protected from enemy action.

Firing Positions

The emphasis on unturreted vehicles using clever firing positions and ambush tactics is something that comes up time and again. One engineer report on the use of Nashorns said:

> Fire lanes, which were cut into wooded areas to ensure the use of Nashorns from flanking firing positions not suspected by the enemy, proved to be excellent. … These firing lanes often made it possible to destroy the Russian assault guns and tanks standing in front of their own HKL, which felt safe due to the dense forest opposite, and to relieve the infantry. … The development of firing positions at particularly vulnerable points, where the Nashorns had to be dug in, was also only possible with the help of the *Pioniere* platoon deploying explosives

Die Sturmgeschützbatterie of 1942 emphasizes the care needed to pick firing positions. Gun commanders were told to reconnoiter carefully "so that it is possible to open fire immediately after entering the position. It's best if the gun can open fire without being recognized beforehand and it is difficult for the enemy to determine the location of the gun during firing." Firing positions should meet the following requirements:

> 1. The firing position should be as hidden as possible. The gun should not protrude beyond the cover more than absolutely necessary. Positions in hollows, behind dams and mounds of earth are ideal.
>
> 2. It should be as perpendicular to the enemy's direction as possible so that the gun is not hit in its vulnerable flank.
>
> 3. It should be located so that it can be fired from at the main combat distances. Firing positions that are too far away will impair the hit rate; if they are pushed too far forward, the lateral field of aim is too small.

Ambush tactics: with only 12° of traverse, the *Sturmgeschütz* was better employed from ambush than in the open. Here, a camouflaged ambush position: ideally there would be a preplanned escape route at the rear. (SA-kuva/Finnish Archives)

4. The flight path must not be interrupted by the terrain, as this would endanger your own infantry from early explosions.

5. Steep slopes should be avoided, as the gun would then present its vulnerable lower side to the enemy and the depth of aim might not be sufficient.

6. If neither the terrain nor the ground cover lend themselves to a favorable firing position, it may be advisable to initially choose a covered ambush position during the attack, from which one can break out at the appropriate moment to open fire, in the manner of the starting position for an assault.

Once the firing position has been reconnoitered, the next problem is to take it up without being seen so that it works as an ambush position. It's important to be able to stay hidden taking up the position until the first shot is fired. The following should be observed:

1. When driving into the first firing position, preparations are made to such an extent that no further instructions are required during the advance. During the attack, the gun commander must be able to identify the next, favorable firing position from the previous position, and at the latest when driving forward, and instruct the assault gun driver to do so. Direction points are a good aid for this. If this is not possible, he must influence the driver's steering movements by shouting or using signals.

2. If areas that can be seen must be driven through, they must be crossed quickly.

3. If possible, only drive perpendicular to the enemy's direction. About 10 m before the new firing position, the gun should already be in the direction required to open fire. Steering movements in the firing position should be avoided. … The assault gun should always remain in its firing position until all targets that can be seen from there have been attacked. Only then is a change of position justified. A premature retreat to cover may only take place if the assault gun is threatened with immediate destruction by weapons against which it cannot defend itself, or if the assault gun has run out of ammunition or is no longer operational for other reasons.

Conclusion

The German Army of World War II was a horse-drawn army. Significant numbers of personnel and supplies had to be used to keep the horses in the field and working hard. They were slower than vehicles and a lot of them were needed to pull things that engines found easy.

On the other hand, armored fighting vehicles, particularly those that carried a big gun, were a relatively new and untried commodity. There had been few opportunities to work them out—how big they should be, what equipment they needed, how to handle their logistics, and how they should be used. World War II was the proving ground for the tank, self-propelled artillery, and the assault gun.

There was a lot of trial and error and few countries got it right first time but there's a case for saying that the *Sturmgeschütz* was one of the few World War II projects that really did work. More reliable than most, as an assault gun it was just what the infantry wanted; as a *Panzerjäger* its results speak for themselves. It proved a stable platform for upgunning with the long L/48 main gun and went on to be linked with as many as 30,000 tank kills. Above all, like the best of the Allied vehicles, it was straightforward to manufacture and was built in quantity.

That can't be said of the many other bigger and bigger machines that took German production away from the workmanlike into the realm of fantasy. The continuous search for the bigger and best—the Hornisse, Sturmtiger, Jagdtiger, Maus—meant that German AFV production, under increasing aerial harassment, never had a chance to produce the number of vehicles it needed. Despite brilliant tactics, training, optics, and guns, the Germans were unable to beat the mass-produced but efficiently resourced Allied armor.

And through it all were the crews, who had to think like infantry while acting like artillerymen. Their role as *Sturmartillerie* was multifaceted, requiring the ability of a gunner, the wherewithal of a *Panzermann*, the infantry awareness of a *Panzergrenadier*, plus a fair dose of *I-Dienste* maintenance knowledge, coupled with tactical astuteness, leadership ability, initiative, and communications skills. The manuals weren't written when the first SPGs rolled off the production lines, and in many cases the crews learned on the job, at all times underwritten by resourcefulness and bravery.

It's fitting that part of the monument "Explosion," erected in 1981 near Volokolamsk, should be a StuG III Ausf D—reconstructed by Dmitry Bushmakow—as it was the most numerous of the German tracked weapons that fought in the Soviet Union. (Otpolzaj/WikiCommons/CC BY-SA 3.0)

Further Reading

Anderson, Thomas. *Panzerartillerie Firepower for the Panzer Divisions*. Osprey, 2019.

Anderson, Thomas. *Sturmgeschütz: Panzer, Panzerjäger, Waffen-SS and Luftwaffe Units 1943–45*. Osprey, 2017.

Anderson, Thomas. *The History of the Panzerjäger 1: Origins and Evolution 1939–42*, and *2: From Stalingrad to Berlin 1943–45*. Osprey, 2018/20.

Baxter, Ian. *Waffen-SS Armour on the Eastern Front 1941–1945*. Pen & Sword Military, 2021.

Bork, Bruno. *STUG III Brigade 191: The Buffalo Brigade*. Greenhill Books, 2021.

Buffetaut, Yves. *German Armor in Normandy*. Casemate Publishers, 2018

Carruthers, Bob. *Stürmgeschutze: Armoured Assault Guns*. Pen & Sword Military, 2013.

Chamberlain, Peter, & Hilary L. Doyle. *Encyclopedia of German Tanks of World War II*. A&AP, 1978.

Davis, Brian L. *German Army Uniforms and Insignia 1933–1945*. Brockhampton Press, 1998.

Doyle, Hilary Louis, & Thomas L. Jentz. *Panzer Tracts Various*. Panzerwrecks Ltd.

Feenstra, Jon. *Panzerjäger on the Battlefield*. PeKo Publishing, 2017.

FM17-12 *Armored Force Field Manual Tank Gunnery*. U.S. War Department, April 22, 1943.

Friedli, Lukas. *Repairing the Panzers Vols 1 & 2*. Panzerwrecks, 2010, 2011.

Friesen, Bruno. *Panzer Gunner*. Helion, 2008.

Kast, Bernhard (Ed). *STUG Ausbildung, Einsatz und Führung der Sturmgeschützbatterie*. Military History Group, 2023.

Laugier, Didier *Sturmartillerie Volume 2*. Heimdal, 2011.

Liedtke, Gregory. *Enduring the Whirlwind: The German Army and the Russo-German war 1941–1943*. Wolverhampton Military Studies No. 21, Helion, 2022.

Michaelis, R. *Deutsche Kriegsauszeichnungen 1939–1945*. Dörfler Verlag, 2007.

Mueller-Hillebrand, General Burkhart H. *German Report Series: German Tank Maintenance in World War II*. Department of the Army, 1954.

Nachrichtenblatt der Panzertruppen, various issues.

Niehorster, Leo W. G. *German World War II Organizational series*, various. The Military Press.

Sander, Friedrich. *Blood, Dust and Snow Diaries of a Panzer Commander in Germany and on the Eastern Front 1938–1943*. Greenhill Books, 2022.

Schneider, Wolfgang. *Panzer Tactics: German Small-Unit Armor Tactics in World War II*. Stackpole, 2006.

Seidler, Hans. *Hitler's Tank Killer: Sturmgeschütz at War 1940–1945*. Pen & Sword Military, 2010.

Spielberger, Walter J., & Hilary L. Doyle. *Beute-Kfz und Panzer der Wehrmacht Vollkettenfahrzeuge*. Motorbuch Verlag, 2016.

Stoves, Rolf. *Die 22. Panzer Division, 25. Panzer Division, 27. Panzer Division und die 233. Reserve Panzer-Division*. Podzun-Pallas-Verlag, 1985.

Számvéber, Norbert. *Illustrated History of the Sturmgeschütz-Abteilung 202*. Peko, 2016.

Tiquet, Pierre. *German Tank Destroyers*. Casemate Publishers, 2021.

TM-E30-451 *Handbook on German Military Forces, 15 March 1945*. U.S. Army, 1945.

Tucker-Jones, Anthony. *German Assault Guns and Tank Destroyers 1940–1945*. Pen & Sword Military, 2016.

Zaloga, Stephen J. *New Vanguard 298: German Tanks in Normandy 1944*, and, *318: Tanks in Operation Bagration 1944*. Osprey, 2021/23.

Index

Alkett (Altmärkische Kettenfabrik GmbH), 4–7, 12, 15–16, 18, 20, 22, 33, 55, 58, 60, 66–67, 73, 110
Altengrabow, 31
ammunition, 8–9, 14–15, 22, 26, 33–34, 36, 59, 61, 63, 69–71, 73, 77–81, 90, 92, 94, 97–98, 103, 109–10, 118, 123, 125
Arracourt, battle of, 22, 26
awards & decorations, 38, 42, 48, 49, 50, 51

Balkan campaign, 4, 13
Baukommando Becker, 18
Becker, Alfred, 24, 64, 110
Berlin, and battle for, 4, 12, 20, 28, 31, 33–35, 68, 100
Brauchitsch, Walther von, 11, 49
British & Commonwealth forces, 13–14, 23, 26
British tanks, conversion of, 17, 110
Budapest, battles for, 26, 50

Cherkassy Pocket, 35
crew duties & positions, 9, 13, 36, 43, 54, 58–59, 63, 69, 79, 88–102

Daimler-Benz, 4, 11
Demyansk salient, 49
Deutsche Eisenwerke, 6, 22
Die Sturmgeschützbatterie, 80, 124

El Alamein, battles of, 14–15, 18
Epinal, 35

Falaise Pocket/Gap, 23, 25
French tanks, conversion of, 18, 60–61, 64, 110
Friesen, Bruno, 32, 35–36, 93, 99
Fritsch, Werner von, 10–11

Gazala, battles of, 13–14
Guderian, Heinz Günther, 46
Guderian, Heinz, 11–12, 18–20, 108, 118
Günther, Alfred, 32

Heereswaffenamt (Army Weapons Office, HWA), 11
Henschel, 5, 71
Hitler, Adolf, 4, 6–7, 19–20, 22, 26, 28, 49–50

Instandsetzungsdienste (*I-Dienste*), 115, 122–23, 126

Kasserine Pass, battle of, 13–14
Kharkov, third battle of, 10, 19, 51, 55, 63, 65
Krupp, 4, 6–7, 11, 20, 58
Kubinka Tank Museum *also* Patriot Museum, 70–71, 74–75, 86, 109
Kurland Peninsula, battles for, 25, 51
Kursk, battle of *see also Unternehmen Zitadelle*, 7, 20, 22, 77, 108, 110

Manstein, Erich von, 4, 10–11, 16
Metaxas Line (Greece), 13, 34
Model, Walter, 4, 45

Nachrichtenblatt der Panzertruppen, 36, 122
Nazi Party, 30, 50, 104
Normandy campaign, 22–23, 25–26, 32, 69, 84, 110
Nova-Technik GmbH (Notek night-driving device), 53, 57, 74, 102
NSKK (National Socialist Motor Transport Corps), 30

OKH (Oberbefehlshaber des Heeres), 33, 36, 116
Operations: Allied—*Bluecoat*, 23, 26; *Crusader*, 14; *Goodwood*, 64; *Market Garden*, 22; *Torch*, 15
German *Unternehmen*: *Barbarossa*, 4, 16, 35, 38, 52, 60, 73, 106, 113; *Fall Blau*, 16; *Seelöwe*, 13; *Sonnenblume*, 14; *Wacht am Rhein*, 26, 107
Ostketten, 99, 117

Parola Armor Museum, 90, 99
Polish campaign, 11, 24, 38, 79, 102, 109
Porsche, 20, 107
Prague, 31, 34–35, 66

Red Army, 20, 23, 25, 27, 34, 48, 100, 103, 118
Rheinmetall-Borsig AG, 4, 12

Saint-Martin-du-Bois, fight at, 23, 26
School of Tank Technology (UK), 14, 54
Smolensk, 38, 51, 105
Spranz, Bodo, 38
Stalingrad, battle of, 18–19, 23, 50, 56, 109
Sturmgeschütze, Panzerjäger & *Panzerartillerie* (all Ausf): "Dicker Max," 4; Ferdinand/Elefant, 6–7, 17, 19–21, 32, 69, 71, 78, 88–89, 107–8; Grille, 5–6, 22, 24–26, 39, 73, 76–77, 79, 110; Hornisse/Nashorn, 6, 8, 16, 19, 21–22, 25, 27, 32, 66, 69–70, 78, 80, 88–89, 107–8, 124, 126; Hummel, 22, 25–26, 32, 40, 66, 77, 79, 80–82, 110, 116; Jagdpanther, 7, 9, 17, 21, 23, 26–27, 68–69, 78, 84, 89, 107–8, 114, 116; Jagdpanzer 38(t) (Hetzer), 7, 9, 21, 26, 32, 34–35, 37, 61, 66, 78, 85–86, 88–89, 106–7; Jagdpanzer IV, 4, 7, 9, 17, 21, 23, 26, 34, 66, 78, 86, 88–89, 98–99, 107–8, 122–24; Jagdtiger, 7, 9, 13, 17, 21–22, 27, 32, 69, 72, 78, 88–89, 107–8, 116, 126; Marder 38(t), 16, 61; Marder I, 16–17, 25, 60, 64, 109; Marder II, 5, 15–18, 25, 62–63; Marder III, 5–6, 14–18, 25, 28, 48, 61, 65, 78, 86, 88–89, 106; Maus, 126; Panzerjäger 38(t), 16, 23; Panzerjäger I, 4, 13–14, 17, 24, 40, 47, 61, 88–89, 106, 119; sIG 33 auf Fahrgestell PzKpfw II (Sf) (Sturmpanzer III), 24, 73; StuG 40, 4, 6, 12, 18, 29, 38, 42, 45, 55–56, 58, 85–86, 92, 98, 100, 104, 112, 116; StuG III, 4–7, 12–13, 19, 21–23, 25, 32–34, 37, 52–54, 56–59, 73, 78, 80, 87–89, 104–7, 109, 111–14, 116, 126; StuG IV, 7, 13, 20, 27, 34–35, 37, 58–59, 66, 104, 106, 116; Sturmgeschütz, 10, 13, 52; Sturmhaubitze 42 (StuH), 5–6, 12, 22, 25, 32, 58–59, 104; Sturm-Infanteriegeschütz 33B (Sturmpanzer II), 24, 73; Sturmpanzer I Bison, 22, 24, 73, 110, 123; Sturmpanzer IV (Brummbär), 6, 22, 24–25, 73, 105; Sturmtiger, 22, 24–25, 75, 126; Wespe, 5–6, 22, 24–25, 29, 32, 75, 77, 79–80, 82, 84, 110

tactics, 31, 35–37, 118–26
training & *Schulen*, 13, 21, 23, 30–40, 50, 71, 90–93, 105, 108–9, 124, 126
Truppenübungsplätze (training areas): Böhmen, 35; Mielau, 34

uniforms, 38–48, 50–51, 85, 104
U.S. Army, 13–14, 26–27, 45–47, 51, 61, 66, 121

Vistula River, 25, 28

Wehrmacht, 4, 25, 28, 30, 36, 40, 84, 87, 112; Army/Heer, 8, 13, 16, 24–25, 39, 43, 49, 60, 78, 111, 118, 120, 126; *Artillerie*, 22, 30–31, 35, 37, 51, 103; Luftwaffe, 39, 44, 62, 85, 113; *Panzerwaffe*, 11, 18, 22, 31, 66, 122; *Sturmartillerie*, 3, 10–11, 15, 31–32, 35–43, 45, 69, 103–5, 126; *Ostheer*, 16, 18; Waffen-SS, 5, 35, 44, 47, 49, 75, 104
Winterketten, 116–17
Wittmann, Michael, 32